闽南师范大学学术著作出版专项经费资助

新锐
经管学术系列

中国普惠金融
可持续性研究

郝晋辉 著

厦门大学出版社 国家一级出版社
XIAMEN UNIVERSITY PRESS 全国百佳图书出版单位

图书在版编目(CIP)数据

中国普惠金融可持续性研究:英文/郝晋辉著.—厦门:厦门大学出版社,2019.3
(新锐经管学术系列)
ISBN 978-7-5615-7329-7

Ⅰ.①中⋯　Ⅱ.①郝⋯　Ⅲ.①金融事业－经济可持续发展－研究－中国－英文
Ⅳ.①F832

中国版本图书馆 CIP 数据核字(2019)第 043070 号

出 版 人	郑文礼
责任编辑	江珏玙
封面设计	蒋卓群
技术编辑	许克华

出版发行 厦门大学出版社

社　　址	厦门市软件园二期望海路 39 号
邮政编码	361008
总 编 办	0592-2182177　0592-2181406(传真)
营销中心	0592-2184458　0592-2181365
网　　址	http://www.xmupress.com
邮　　箱	xmup@xmupress.com
印　　刷	厦门市金凯龙印刷有限公司

开本	720 mm×1 000 mm　1/16
印张	10.75
字数	206 千字
插页	2
版次	2019 年 3 月第 1 版
印次	2019 年 3 月第 1 次印刷
定价	38.00 元

本书如有印装质量问题请直接寄承印厂调换

厦门大学出版社
微信二维码

厦门大学出版社
微博二维码

Preface

Since it was first purposed by the United Nations in 2005, inclusive finance has enjoyed rapid growth in the world. In recent years, the sustainability of inclusive finance has become an important issue. At the same time, in the era of big data, the situation of institutional constraints and asymmetric information faced by the entire financial system has been eased, and the foundation of financial repression has been loosened. The global pattern of inclusive finance is facing the impacts of internet economy and internet finance. In this context, the development of inclusive finance faces more opportunities and challenges for its sustainability.

This paper aims at investigating the development and sustainability of inclusive finance in China and outlining the features and importance of inclusive finance in the context of the urban-rural dual structure and the urbanization process in China. This paper argues that the sustainable development of inclusive finance in China shows Chinese characteristics; it is related to the process of urbanization in China and is subject to the urban-rural dual structure. The sustainable development of inclusive finance in China has the following features: development stages to be improved, unbalanced development between the East and the West, and segmentation in financial markets. Based on these characteristics of the times, this paper conducted an FSS analysis on China's inclusive financial institutions, drawing the conclusion that the financial sustainability of China's Internet financial platforms is relatively good. The study of this paper also found that the government's influence and control over inclusive finance in China are unique in the world, leading to the fast development of China's inclusive finance. Still, China's inclusive finance is troubled by the problems of poor supervision.

Countries in Southeast Asia show different levels of development of inclusive finance. Among them, the Philippine's NGO "Center for Agriculture and Rural Development (CARD)" has enabled women in poverty-stricken areas to achieve economic independence and contributed to building a more stable social and economic base. Indonesia has adopted the mode of providing inclusive financial services by state-owned banks. They have accumulated certain experience and lessons in the development of inclusive finance which are worth learning from.

The innovations of this paper are as follows. First, the paper analyzed the financial data of China's current inclusive financial companies under the theoretical framework of the global financial inclusion system and reached reasonable conclusions. Second, the development of inclusive finance in China has its own particularities, such as the urban-rural dual structure, the advancement of financial technology, etc. This paper has combined these characteristics to ensure that the analysis of sustainability is of practical importance. Third, this paper compared the inclusive financial sustainability of China with that of two Southeast Asian countries with similar externalities in search of general characteristics and specific issues so as to arrive at effective conclusions and policy recommendations for the sustainable development of inclusive finance in China. Besides, the paper also provided a preliminary analysis of the preconditions and foundations of inclusive finance development in these countries, and compared their similarities and differences in regard to their applications for China.

It should be admitted that this paper's research has certain deficiencies. The Chinese government has served as a strong driver in the development of financial inclusion which is short but rapid. With the speed of economic development and government regulation, the development of inclusive finance in China is facing the uncertainty of the external environment. This paper did not analyze the sustainability of China's inclusive finance in the context of the Chinese system, but set the presupposition that the existing inclusive financial policies would maintain certain policy continuity. Therefore, the research may fail to analyze the sustainability of inclusive finance in regard to policy variables and long-term effectiveness as the proposed policy recommendations are unable to adapt to the changing policy environment.

CONTENTS

Chapter 1 Introduction

1.1 Topic Selection Background

1.1.1 Development of Inclusive Finance in the World

The emergence of inclusive finance was originated from 1970s when Prof. Yunus in Bangladesh started microcredit and founded Grameen Bank providing financing service to poor people in rural areas. Since then, microcredit, widely circulated around the world, has given large numbers of financially excluded people access to previously unavailable financial services (Leyshon, 1993; Thrift, 1995)[1]. At first, the development of inclusive finance was not extensive, and the research on it was at how to carry out and develop inclusive finance, mostly focusing on its availability, loanability and its service quality. Those studies played a positive role in the development of inclusive finance.

The concept of inclusive finance advocates a comprehensive approach of providing universal financial services to all groups and sectors of the society, especially to the poor and low-income groups, so that everyone has the opportunity to participate in economic development and to achieve common prosperity. Therefore, as soon as it appeared, inclusive finance showed a rapid global growth like a prairie fire caused

---

① Jiao Jinpu. Building China's Inclusive Finance System[M]. China Financial Publishing House,18.

by a single spark[①]. In 2006, the United Nations set up the goal of inclusive finance as that each developing country should have a complete system of financial institutions under a sound policy, legal and regulatory framework that will jointly provide suitable financial products and services to all levels of people.

Since the Asian Financial Crisis in 1997, the traditional foreign investment-dependent economy of Southeast Asia has suffered a heavy setback, and the currency rates in these countries have depreciated remarkably. Every country in the world has seen various different levels of the impact. With political unrest and huge gap between the rich and the poor, there has been increasing concern over assistance to the poor. The traditional public welfare service for the poor, however, shows low sustainability considering the over-burdened government finance, giving way to inclusive finance which has been seriously attended around the world at this stage.

After the outbreak of American sub-prime mortgage crisis and the Occupy Wall Street movement[②], countries around the world have felt the need to rethink their existing financial models, among which inclusive finance is favored due to its emphasis on the inclusiveness of finance. Then inclusive finance has gained extensive attention as a rising star in the financial system after the European Debt Crisis, and has been regarded as an important financial means to ease and avoid crisis, as it is an essential component of a country's mainstream financial system and can provide high-quality financial services to meet the financial

---

① Brigit Helms. Access for All[M]. CGAP,9.

② Occupy Wall Street (OWS) was a protest movement that began on September 17, 2011, in Zuccotti Park, located in New York City's Wall Street financial district, receiving global attention and spawning a surge in the movement against economic inequality worldwide.

demand of the masses, particularly those in poorer and less accessible regions, reducing the cost for both customers and service providers.

1.1.2 Development of Inclusive Finance in China

From 2004 to 2010, the Chinese government issued out the Central Document No.1 in consecutive 6 years, mentioning the Chinese financial system, especially how to support and develop inclusive finance in China. Since then under the impetus of external forces, inclusive finance has developed fast in China and led to a wide coverage of various inclusive finance forms such as microcredit in banking financial institutions, government-funded poverty alleviation agencies, NGOs and microcredit companies, pawn shops and guarantee companies, petty insurance, etc. However, it was not until the 3rd plenary session of the 18th Central Committee of the Communist Party of China in 2013 that China really paid more attention on this concept when "Develop Inclusive Finance, Encourage Financial Innovation, Enrich Financial Market Hierarchy and Products" (Part Ⅲ, Article 12) was officially addressed[1].

In 2013, the economy growth in the U.S. slowed down, the Euro zone economy continued to shrink, prices constantly rose in Brazil, Russia and India, the appreciation of bitcoin was nearly a hundred times, and the world economy entered an unstable climate. China proposed many measures such as "expanding domestic demand" to promote steady economic growth. After President Xi Jinping took office, he put forward the slogan "Empty talk is harmful to the nation, while doing practical work will make it thrive."[2] These measures can be traced to

---

① http://www.czwsda.org.cn/lmnr/qck.asp? id=317.
② http://news.cntv.cn/china/20121201/101570.shtml

the same origin, that is, China's inclusive finance serves for the actual economic development in China, which is the purpose of the top design. In fact, China proposed "developing inclusive finance" in order to better support its real economy, let finance follow the mass lines to allow all citizens to have the opportunities to enjoy more financial services[①]. In this way, through different means the Chinese inclusive finance achieve the same goal as the international inclusive finance set its purpose.

2014 is the year of transformation for Chinese internet finance, also is a fast growth year for inclusive finance in China. The State moderately relaxed market access and encouraged the financial sector to carry out organizational innovation, product innovation and model innovation so as to continuously improve the role of inclusive financial institutions. In particular, financial support for small and micro-enterprises was strengthened and the financing structure for small and micro-enterprises was improved. Because small and micro-enterprises are the main body of entrepreneurship and innovation, providing inclusive financial services to them matches the goal of inclusive finance. On March. 5, 2015, at the 3rd session of the 12th NPC, Premier Li Keqiang pointed out in his work report that in 2015, the government would step up the construction of a multi-level capital market system and vigorously develop inclusive finance. Li Keqiang said, in that year, the government would implement stock issuance registration system reform, develop regional equity markets to serve the SMEs, promote the securitization of credit assets, expand the issuance scale of corporate bonds, develop financial derivative market, introduce catastrophe insurance and individual tax-deferred endowment insurance, innovate financial supervision, prevent and

---

① Zhang Zhengpin. Study on the Sustainability of MFIs in China, 3.

resolve financial risks so as to let all market players share the benefits of financial services[①].

When discussing the development of inclusive finance in China, it is necessary to put it in the context of China's Urbanization and Urban-rural Dual Structure. China is now in the process of long-term urbanization, and China's economic structure has obvious characteristics of urban-rural dual structure. The process of urbanization in China is really fast. In this dynamic process, the different economic characteristics of the east and the west also affect the different characteristics of China's inclusive finance, thas the supply and demand of inclusive financial institutions in urban and rural areas are different. At the same time, China as a country with a socialist market economy[②] is in the process of a long-term economic growth. Thus, this paper aims to analyze and discuss the sustainability of inclusive finance in China under the background of urbanization and high-speed economic development.

1.1.3 Development of Inclusive Finance in Indonesia and the Philippines

Indonesia, the Philippines and China have some similarities in economic structure and both have experienced export-oriented economic strategies. In 1997, after the Asian financial crisis, these two Southeast Asian countries made a series of adjustments to the economic structure of the export-dependent economy, and inclusive finance gradually developed in this environment. Whereas in China at this time, the economic

---

① http://www.chinanews.com/gn/2017/03—05/8165806.shtml

② Zou Lixing, Developmental Finance and Sustainable Development, Hunan University Press

development was relatively slow. The development of inclusive finance in Indonesia and the Philippines started earlier than that in China, and thus their experience has vital importance in the study of the sustainability of inclusive finance in China. Therefore, this article intends to clearly judge the current developmental stage of China's inclusive finance and estimate the direction of the sustainable development of China's inclusive finance through a comparative analysis of the sustainability of inclusive finance in Indonesia, the Philippines and China.

1.1.4 Prominent Issue of the Sustainability of Inclusive Finance

Since the concept of inclusive finance was proposed and promoted by the United Nations in 2005, the studies on inclusive finance mainly focused on the initial stages of research, such as its availability, loanability and service quality, later the construction of its relevant system became a research focus, that is compatible with the beginning and proliferation of inclusive finance in the world. With the popularization and promotion of inclusive finance in the world, the concept of inclusive finance has gradually been accepted by all countries, it has also experienced rapid development for more than ten years. After a large number of inclusive financial institutions engaged in this business, inclusive finance itself has also presented a series of problems such as institutional loss, mismatch of risks and returns in the market and the impact of political environment, etc. The inclusive finance in China and the world is now all facing this challenge of how to reach sustainable and stable development. In response to this question, the sustainability of inclusive finance has gradually become an important research topic.

Previous studies on inclusive finance sustainability primarily fo-

cused on the financial sustainability of the inclusive financial institutions, that is, how an inclusive financial institution can maintain a basic
operating status through its business with healthy financial indicators[①].

However, inclusive finance is a systematic concept. Inclusive financial institutions are only an important part of the inclusive financial system, which will be unsustainable without other parts. Thus, this paper
attempts to study the sustainability of inclusive finance from the perspective of the entire inclusive financial system, recognizing that inclusive finance is part of a larger system and environment and relies on the
joint effect of inclusive financial system and external factors as well as
the synergy of the partial and the whole inclusive financial system to
maintain and ensure its sustainability. External market factors, political
factors, government regulation and cultural factors all have an impact
on the sustainability of inclusive finance[②].

For China, since the United Nations advocated inclusive finance a
decade ago, the overall development of inclusive finance in the country
has been impressive. However, how to maintain and even develop inclusive finance is a common issue faced by China and the whole world. The
sustainability of inclusive finance is the result of the development and
maturity of inclusive finance, and the problem of its sustainability does
not stand out in the initial and developmental stage.

Inclusive finance has both inclusive and financial features, that is,
the dual goals of inclusiveness and finance. In the initial stage, due to
inadequate market development, less fierce competition and powerful
government supports, the inclusive and financial features, or the dual

---

①　refers to the institutions' accounting profit when revenues exceed spending.

②　Zhong Wei. Evaluation and Analysis of the Sustainable Development of China's Finance[M]. Economic Science Press,36.

goals show certain overlap (Creason, 2004). Therefore, in these stages, the conflict between the dual goals is not intense; rather, they promote each other. However, in the meantime, the conflict between the dual goals of inclusive finance is very prominent, which is reflected in the self — sustaining of the inclusive financial system, that is, after gradual independence from external forces and old paths, inclusive finance will through the utilization of self-commercialization maintain its results and realize financially and organizationally sustainable development (Du Xiaoshan, 2015)[①]. Thus, this paper intends to measure the degree of the deviation of the dual goals to clarify the major contradictions of the sustainability issue.

The issues of the sustainability of inclusive finance are mainly manifested in two aspects. On the one hand, the requirements of financial features of inclusive finance can not be satisfied if China tries to meet the inclusive goal. On the other hand, inclusive finance will deviate from its inclusive goal and return to the path of traditional finance and be virtually beyond the scope of inclusive finance if China tries to maintain the financial sustainability of financial institutions. Therefore, the essential issue regarding the sustainability of inclusive finance is to ensure that the inclusive and financial goals of inclusive finance are achieved at the same time without deviation.

1.2 Research Significance

The study on the sustainability of inclusive finance in China has

---

① Cheng Enjiang. China's non — governmental microfinance and rural finance[M]. Zhejiang University Press, 5.

both theoretical and realistic significance. In 2012, China promised that it would lift its population out of poverty by 2020, in which inclusive finance would play an important role. Thus, studies on inclusive finance will contribute to the realization of the fundamental purpose of inclusive finance.

Firstly, the study on the sustainability of inclusive finance in China hopes to introduce to the world the development and characteristics of China's inclusive finance in different stages, and to enrich the research on the development and diversity of inclusive finance in the world.

Secondly, the study on the sustainability of inclusive finance in China analyzed and found the advantages and disadvantages of both sides through comparison between China and Southeast Asian countries, providing a reliable reference and guide in practice.

Thirdly, the study on the sustainability of inclusive finance in China analyzed the specific economic stages and economic structures of China, which has important practical significance in overcoming poverty, accelerating urbanization, and changing and improving the urban—rural dual economic structure in China.

1.3 Definition of Related Concepts

1.3.1 Inclusive Finance

In this paper, inclusive finance is a financial form that achieves the goal of inclusiveness through financial means, of which the short-term goal is to narrow the gap between the rich and the poor, to avoid the financial crisis, to improve financial equity, to reduce financial exclusion and to increase financial inclusiveness and the long-term goal is to increase GNI and improve social welfare. The "Development Plan for Promoting Inclusive Finance (2016—2020)" issued by the State Council has made a clear definition of inclusive finance as well as its coverage and development goals. According to the Plan, Inclusive finance refers to financial services offered by financial institutions to micro-businesses, farmers, low-income population in urban areas, poor population, the disabled, and senior citizens. The goal is to set an inclusive finance system that is in coordination with the construction of a moderately prosperous society by 2020 and satisfies people's need for financial services.

According to UN's definition, inclusive finance should have such characteristics:

(1) all households and businesses are able to access a range of financial services at reasonable prices, including savings, short-term and long-term loans, leasing, agency, mortgages, insurance, pensions, payments, local remittances and international remittances, etc.;

(2) there are sound institutions that follow reasonable internal management systems, industry performance standards and market surveillance mechanisms and accept reasonable prudential supervision;

(3) it should be equipped with financial and institutional sustainability capabilities, which lay the foundation for the institutions to provide long—term, continuous financial services;

(4) there should be a diverse range of financial service providers who provide customers with a variety of financial services that are cost-effective and viable when feasible.

The United Nations' definition of inclusive finance focuses on its e-quality and inclusiveness. The definition of inclusive finance in China, on the other hand, includes the requirements for the sustainability of inclusive finance, that is, the inclusive financial system should continue to effectively and continuously provide financial services to the key vulnerable groups under the premise of meeting the principles of equal opportunity and commercial sustainability. Specifically, the sustainability of inclusive finance refers to: (1) Affordability. The providers in the inclusive financial systems should be able to bear the costs when providing financial services, the demanders should be able to pay the consideration, and the two parties should be able to bear the costs on a certain basis to compensate for the loss of efficiency caused by externalities. (2) Comprehensiveness. The sustainability of China's inclusive financial services has reaffirmed the need to provide appropriate and effective financial services to all groups in the society with non-exclusive purposes. Therefore, the comprehensive coverage reflects the purpose of inclusive finance in achieving the sustainable goals. (3) Equality of opportunity. It embodies the fairness of inclusive finance.

Inclusive finance has internal conflicts, because inclusiveness belongs to the idea of social welfare and is people-oriented, while finance is benefit-oriented and utilitarianism in the institutional trend is determined by the nature of finance. The result of the conflict is financial unfairness and exclusion, making financially vulnerable groups such as low-income population, farmers, middle and small-sized business owners unable to get financial services and producing resistance and rejection. In recent years, the so-called inclusive growth has been aimed at bringing this population into the financial system.

1.3.2 The urban-rural dual economic structure

The urban-rural dual economic structure generally refers to the coexistence of the urban economy characterized by socialized production

and the rural economy characterized by small-scale agricultural production. The urban-rural dual economic structure in China is mainly manifested as follows:

(1) the urban economy is dominated by modern large-scale industrial production while the rural economy is dominated by typical small-
scale agricultural economy;

(2) the urban infrastructure such as roads, communication, sanita-
tion and education is well developed while the rural infrastructure is
poor;

(3) the per capita consumption level of urban areas is much higher
than that of rural areas;

(4) compared with urban population, the rural population is quite
large.

1.4 Aims of this Study

Inclusive finance has been widely studied in the financial field. Yet,
few studies have explored the sustainability of inclusive finance. More
specifically, the sustainability of inclusive finance in China has not yet
been widely studied.

Hence, this article aims at investigating the sustainability of inclusive finance in China based on the sustainability of inclusive finance
from both the static and the dynamic prospective as well as China's national conditions, experience and lessons of Indonesia and the Philippines, which will be elaborated on in the following chapters. This dis-
sertation tries answer the following two questions:

- RQ1: Is the development of inclusive finance in China sustainable?

• RQ2: How to promote the sustainability of inclusive finance in China?

1.5 Methodology

This paper mainly uses the method of quantitative analysis and qualitative study, and in addition, adopts the following methods:

(1)Literature Research: obtain the theoretical basis and realizability of the theories studied in this paper through the review of relevant literature at home and abroad from the time dimension.

(2) Quantitative Analysis: use Stata and a combined analytical method of qualitative and mathematical analysis; conduct a qualitative analysis of the general dynamic condition of the sustainability of inclusive finance; conduct an analysis of important factors in the index test of inclusive finance and obtain important factors and indicators of the sustainability of inclusive finance in its different stages.

(3)Comparative Research: compare the strengths and weaknesses of inclusive finance in China and the major countries in Southeast: Indonesia and the Philippines.

(4)Case Study by Combining Theory with Practice: analyses the impetus and resistance produced by the division of labor, financial deepening, financial development and Coase theorem, and comprehensively integrate these relations into the system of inclusive financial sustainability for further analysis; analyze the Indonesian People's Bank and other successful and unsuccessful cases of inclusive financial development in other countries based on Internet finance and other theories.

1.6 Innovation and Deficiencies

Based on the existing research on the sustainable development of inclusive finance, this article hopes to make three innovations:

(1) This paper examined the sustainability of the inclusive finance in China under the existing theoretical framework, obtaining relatively new FSS data of China's inclusive financial platforms to investigate the sustainability of China's inclusive finance at the current stage.

(2) Existing literature has explored the development of inclusive finance in developing market economies, however, limited studies have examined the inclusive finance in China within its special contexts and changing conditions. Therefore, this paper aims to narrow this gap by looking carefully into China's special economic background and social conditions such as urban-rural dual structure, urbanization, emerging internet technologies, innovation in insurance, P-to-P and other financial instruments.

(3) This paper compared the sustainability of inclusive finance among different countries, comparing inclusive finance among China and two Southeast Asian countries Indonesia and the Philippines, which share similar external environment with China so as to draw more suitable conclusions and policy recommendations for the sustainable development of inclusive finance in China.

The shortcomings of this study are as follows.

(1) Due to the relatively short and fast development of inclusive finance in China and the strong driving force from the government, China's inclusive finance faces uncertainties from the external environment considering the changes in economic development speed and government

regulation. This article didn't analyze the sustainability of China's inclusive finance in the context of China's system. Instead, it presupposed that the existing inclusive finance policy would maintain certain continuity. Therefore, the study of the sustainability of inclusive finance may not be able to be analyzed under policy variables.

(2)This article didn't study the sustainability of inclusive finance within a boarder dynamic background. Inclusive finance is a branch of finance. As the external technology changes, the cost and income of financial institutions will change. Therefore, there exists the possibility that inclusive finance may be replaced by other financial means or methods. However, this article only analyzed inclusive finance based on existing conditions and prerequisites.

1.7 Literature Review

1.7.1 Review of International Research

The study of the sustainability of inclusive finance, first found in Outlaw and Lane (1994), argued that if microcredit programs were financed entirely through customer savings and loans from formal financial institutions at commercial rates, and if their fees, incomes and interest incomes could fully cover the actual cost of capital, loan loss reserves and operating costs, as well as inflation, then the financial sustainability of inclusive financial institutions would be achieved.

In the early stages of microcredit, expanding outreach to the poor and financially vulnerable groups was the main goal of inclusive finance. In 1998, Ledgewood suggested that MFIs must address two conflicting goals and form two different camps: welfarists and institutionalists.

The welfarists, represented by Dichter, considered the coverage of target customers more important than financial sustainability. Institutionalists, on the other hand, represented by American scholars Sharma and Buchenrieder (2002), thought that the dual goals of microcredit could coexist and were compatible, and only sustainable MFIs could expand their service scope.

The traditional theory held that in the existing financial system, due to innate reasons of financial system itself, there were many people who were excluded from financial services and were totally squeezed out of formal finance. Therefore, in order to allocate funds to the poor through financial market channels, China must innovate and build a new system.

Before the 1980s, subsidized credit paradigm occupied an important position in the theoretical field of rural finance. According to this theory, the agricultural industry had the characteristics of indefinite income, long-term investment and low profitability, so that agriculture would not become the prospective borrower of profit-driven commercial banks. Therefore, in order to alleviate rural poverty, it was necessary to inject funds from the outside and set up special non-profit institutions to allocate funds.

After the 1980s, rural financial systems paradigm emerged. This theory held that the balance between capital supply and demand in rural financial markets should be realized, the interest rates should be determined by the market mechanism, some informal financial institutions in the rural market should be established and maintained, and regular financial institutions and informal financial institutions should be utilized to balance rural financial demand and supply.

In the 1990s, Stiglitz proposed the theory of imperfectly competitive market which argued that the government should supervise imperfectly competitive market such as financial market and intervene in the financial market when appropriate instead of relying solely on the market mechanism to foster the financial market a society needs.

With the increasing commercialization of inclusive finance, commercial capital has entered this area, and the financial sustainability of inclusive finance has been improved. However, this has created the increasingly serious problem of target deviation (Pitt and Khanker, 1999; Morduch, 2000; Karlan and Zinman, 2009), triggering studies on the target deviation of inclusive financial institutions, which mainly focus on the following aspects:

　　(1)definition of target deviation;

　　(2)reasons for target deviation;

　　(3)measurement of target deviation;

　　(4)empirical tests of target deviation;

　　(5)governance of target deviation.

1.7.2 Review of Domestic Research

The current situation of domestic research is mainly reflected in three aspects:

　　(1)the dual goals and innate conflicts of rural financial institutions;

　　(2)the target deviation of microcredit institutions;

　　(3)the governance of target deviation of microcredit institutions.

In the theoretical research, the domestic scholars have mainly studied the necessity and urgency of establishing inclusive finance in terms of its correlation between rural economic development and financial support and achieved the following results.

Xu Xiaobo and Deng Yingtao (1994) analyzed the correlation between rural credit funds and the growth of rural national income. By calculating rural financial-related rate indicators, they showed with graphs and charts that there was a strong correlation between rural credit funds and rural national income.

Luo Enping (2005) argued that rural financial demand could be mainly divided into credit demand, insurance demand, investment and financing demands, etc. And the division was diverse and multilevel with small-scale, high-risk and high-cost characteristics. He advocated the establishment of rural financial risk compensation and dispersion mechanism to promote rural financial innovation and interest rates liberalization process.

According to Deng Li and Ran Guanghe (2006), rural financial scale was the most important indicator of rural economic growth and development. They proposed that to promote rural economic growth, China must increase financial support for agriculture and rural economy and establish coordination mechanism of rural financial and economic development as well as interaction mechanism and funding mechanism.

According to Zhou Guoliang's (2007) study, the current situation of rural finance in China was grim, and the contradictions between supply and demand in rural finance was prominent. The rural financial demand was strong and far greater than supply and it was difficult for farmers to get loans from formal financial institutions.

Li Yaxin (2007) found that rural credit cooperatives, as the mainstay of rural financial services, were raising their awareness of the financial risks of serving agriculture, rural areas and farmers. However, their awareness of expanding credit market failed to keep pace. The design of financial products didn't fully consider the overall demand of farmers, and there was a serious imbalance and dislocation between supply and demand in rural finance.

Zhang Zhiyuan (2009) in his *The Theory of Sustainable Development of Regional Finance* suggested that inclusive finance was an indispensable part of regional finance, and that the sustainability of inclusive finance depended primarily on the overall sustainability of the financial system. Thus the sustainability of inclusive finance should be studied from the perspective of the system and the regional economic and financial sustainability.

Dong Xiaolin and Zhu Minjie (2016) pointed out in the *Building an Inclusive Financial System in Rural China* that inclusive finance was a spontaneous demand in China's rural system which was consistent with the trend of inclusive finance in the world. He mainly analyzed inclusive finance from system designing and held that as soon as inclusive financial system was constructed, it would spontaneously integrate with the original system and function.

In short, the current research at home and abroad has paid attention to the commercialization, risk management and target deviation of inclusive financial institution; still, there exist the following deficiencies:

(1) from the perspective of the research object, foreign studies mainly focus on mature microcredit institutions in countries such as Bolivia and Indonesia, and China's studies on the sustainability of inclusive finance are mainly based on the micro-financial institutions of rural areas: both lack of comprehensive and extensive representativeness.

(2) for the research content, the research on the sustainability of inclusive finance is mainly limited to theoretical research. Foreign scholars have already discussed loan limit, coverage and financial sustain-

ability. However, our research mainly focuses on the specific analysis of certain aspects.

(3)in view of methodology, there are still some limitations in the methods of domestic research, which are mainly theoretical analysis, statistical analysis and case analysis. Compared with the research of international scholars on the risk measurement and target deviation of the sustainability of inclusive financial institutions, domestic research does not pay much attention to the empirical analysis.

(4)from the perspective of the research, the perspective of domestic research needs to be broadened. When studying the sustainability of inclusive finance, it is necessary to consider the impact of macro factors and take external factors into consideration, such as macro systems and market risks as well as external changes caused by insurance and internet technologies.

This article attempts to carry out a comprehensive and in-depth study of the sustainability of inclusive finance in China and aims to gain further results based on the existing research. Considering the different developmental stages of inclusive finance, the introduction of the time dimension will make the study on the sustainability of inclusive finance more targeted to time and space, which will help the study of the overall behavior and framework of the sustainability of inclusive finance.

Chapter 2 Theories and Indicator System of the Study on the Sustainability of Inclusive Finance

2.1 Theories Regarding the Sustainability of Inclusive Finance

2.1.1 Dual Goal Theory of Inclusive Finance's Sustainability

Inclusive financial institutions provide funds and support financial services to the demand side as providers. The institutions are, in fact, the intermediaries of inclusive financial funds and their loan-to-deposit ratios and profits should be in line with the maintenance and sustainable standards of general financial institutions. The sources of risk of inclusive financial institutions are also consistent with those of general financial institutions. However, inclusive finance shows particularity in its risk, as the demand side are mainly microcredit clients who have a single source of incomes and cannot cover their fixed cost expenses with their incomes.

Inclusive financial institutions had the dual goals of inclusiveness and finance at the outset, which were referred to by some scholars as "out reach" and "financial sustainability". In the initial phase, the conflict between the goals of inclusiveness and utilitarianism was not very obvious; or rather, the two promoted each other, that is, inclusive fi-

nancial institutions could not only gain the moral advantages of inclusiveness, creating a moral image different from that of traditional financial institutions, but also acquire commercial monopoly advantages[1],
since at the beginning inclusive financial market formed by financially
excluded people faced less competition and the demand was exceeding
supply. Therefore, inclusive financial institutions could choose relatively high — quality client resources with ease and obtain extremely high
profits.

With the popularization of inclusive finance, more and more inclusive financial institutions and other financial institutions have joined the
inclusive financial services, and the competition has become more and
more fierce. With increasing financial supply and limited resources of
relatively high-quality clients, financial services must be provided to clients in extreme poverty and dire poverty in order to achieve the inclusive goal; however, the profits from these clients can not meet the requirements of financial balance considering the supply costs. At this
time, there is a great deviation between the two goals. It is agreed glob-
ally that MFIs must have the double bottom line of the poor coverage
and financial sustainability, but welfarists and institutionalists have different views on how to balance the double bottom line[2]. Welfarists believe that the coverage of target clients is more important than financial
sustainability, insisting that market-based methods of cost recovery and
subsidy removal would force MFIs to abandon the poor with mis-

---

① Jiao Jinpu. Building China's Inclusive Finance System, 39. It is mentioned that the
types of poverty are divided into three categories: moderate poverty, extreme poverty and dire
poverty. Since inclusive finance could cover the moderately poor group at the beginning, it
didn't have serious problems with benefits and costs.

② Zhang Zhengping. Research on the Sustainable Development of MFIs in China, 22.

matched return and credit risk despite the fact that credit resources can help balance the consumer demand of the poor and increase production, resulting in positive social benefits. One-sidedly pursuing financial sustainability will only increase the burden and vulnerability of the poor and can not deliver the desired effect.

Institutionalists, on the other hand, believe that the dual goals of microcredit are co-existing and compatible, and that only sustainable MFIs can continuously expand their service scope and meet the coverage goals. Schreiner (2002) pointed out that "the society should pay attention to the current and future welfare of the poor, and only self-sustained MFIs can receive strong support for raising social welfare in the long term." Generally speaking, the mainstream opinions in the world accept the beliefs of institutionalists, which the World Bank's Consultative Group for Poverty Alleviation (CGAP) and the U.S. Agency for International Development have both followed and adopted.

2.1.2 Governance Theory of Inclusive Financial: Social Performance Evaluation and Management

Conflict between coverage and financial sustainability are reflected as the imbalance between social and financial performance in actual governance and in fact, an understanding is reached, that is, even if there exist obvious conflicts between the two theoretically, the implementation of performance evaluation and management can effectively coordinate the conflicts and achieve sustainable development, because theoretical conflicts should be placed in specific practice, in which the two sides show little divergence but strong interdependence and indivisibility.

Impact consortium[①] proposed in 2005 that the social performance of small and micro financial institutions was not just a final result, but also a step-by-step process. Therefore, by matching social performance with the known financial performance, the welfare goal would be internalized and deepened in evaluation mechanism. Otherwise, social performance management would be at a disadvantage without the ability to function because unlike the sustainability of financial indicators, it couldn't be quantified.

Table 2.1 Six Dimensions of Social Performance

Dimension	Content
Social mission	Clarity of social mission; Understanding of employee mission; Degree of the completion of social mission.
Coverage	Coverage breadth and depth; Demographics and poverty information of clients; Efforts to cover population lacking financial services.
Employee	Human resources policy; Employee development; Feedback mechanism.
Client service	Efforts to increase client satisfaction; Products and services; Feedback mechanism.

---

① Impact consortium is an international organization that promotes and supports social performance management of MFIs throughout the world.

Continued

Dimension	Content
Connection with neighborhood community	Community and non-financial service projects; Social responsibilities and environmental policies.
Information transparency and consumer protection	Transparent price; Consumer protection policy.

Source: Study on the Sustainable Development of China's MFIs

2.1.3 Dynamic Sustainability Theory of Inclusive Finance

2.1.3.1 Essence of the Sustainability of Inclusive Finance: Dynamic Balance after Financial Deepening

Examining the history of its development, inclusive finance, as part of the larger financial system, has been constantly developing and changing. From a static perspective, as long as the financial sustainability of inclusive financial institutions is maintained, the inclusive financial demand is satisfied, and the market regulation is sound, the sustainability of inclusive finance can be realized. However, this only ensures the sustainability of inclusive finance in its form, neglecting that inclusive finance is the product of financial repression. Once the external conditions of financial repression are lost, there will be no ground for inclusive finance to exist independently.

Financial repression and financial deepening are linked to the characteristics of the developing countries, such as the dual financial structure, low-level monetization, underdeveloped financial market, low efficiency of financial system and the government's strict control over the financial system, etc.

In 1973, Ronald I. McKinnon and Edward S. Shaw put forward the famous "financial repression theory" and "finance deepening theory" after studying the issue of financial development in less developed economies from different angles. McKinnon and Shaw argued that the assumed basis of traditional monetary theory applied only to developed countries, as in developing countries, natural economy takes a large proportion in the overall economy, the degree of economic monetization and commodification is low, and credit instruments are still lacking. The financial market in developing countries are in a separated state, showing a dual financial structure.

Causes for the emergence of the above situation in developing countries are as follows. First, the unsound financial mechanism and underdeveloped financial institutions make it difficult for financial markets to effectively raise social funds. Second, excessive government intervention and regulatory policies in finance have led to "financial repression" which refers to the situation where financial systems with low interest rates, low exchange rates and stagnant economic development coexist.

The interest-rate ceiling formed by financial repression will lead large funds into real capital and tangible assets when inflation heats up, which will inevitably increase inflationary pressures. The government, under the pressure of inflation, usually controls the nominal money supply and drives down the interest rates, which will lead to the outflow of money from the banking system, causing the serious problem of "disintermediation" and forming a vicious circle in economic stagnation.

To promote economic development, the government must lift the financial repression and promote financial deepening. The core of financial deepening is to raise the level of real interest rates and to fully open the financial market for the increase in investment level and investment efficiency. As interest rates rise, the financial intermediation between investors and savers will be strengthened, the intermediary costs will be reduced, and the average ROI and investment structure will be improved, which will have major impacts on income, saving, investment and employment.

Financial repression refers to the policies of government in developing countries to repress financial development. For example, the government strictly controls the financial institutions by stipulating the interest rates of deposits and loans, implementing inflation, depressing real interest rates and adopting a ration system for scarce credit funds. These policies are mainly aimed at the banking system rather than the capital market. Financial deepening theory holds that the financial repression policies will hinder the financial deepening and the improvement of financial efficiency, which is not conducive to economic growth.

With financial repression policies, the government can influence the allocation and utilization of financial resources to support the development of certain industries. Based on the theory established by Johansson and Wang,[1] financial repression restraints the service industry to promote the development of manufacturing industry, which has hindered the changes in the economic structure and resulted in distortions in the economic structure. For example, the allocation of financial funds to the domestic manufacturing industry will lead to the imbalance in the external current account.

Due to the relatively backward technology and underdeveloped international financial market of developing countries, the investment op-

---

[1]　Johansson and Wang in 2011 demonstrated that financial repression leads to structural changes and distortions.

portunities for domestic funds are relatively small. Under such circumstances, FDI provides an effective investment channel for enterprises with relatively abundant capital. Investing in developed countries will help enterprises to obtain industrial upgrading technology; investing in countries with rich resources will help enterprises obtain lower-cost production factors. Therefore, FDI will help enterprises to better promote domestic production and improve the utilization efficiency and ROI.

Vicente Galbis and M.J.Fry supplemented and enriched the MacKinnon and Shaw's theory of financial repression and financial deepening from a different perspective. In "Theory of Financial Intermediaries and Economic Growth in Developing Countries", Galbis analyzed the interest rate policy of less developed countries from the perspective of investment quality. He held that rising rates would allow funds to flow from the inefficient sector to more efficient sectors and raise the overall quality of investment. Whereas Frye argued that the excessive demand for funds caused by low interest rates would lead to non-price rationing; as a result, economic behavior would be distorted, and that higher interest rates would reduce the demand of low-income investors for investment funds and raise the average ROI.

In *Economic Development*, U.S. economists Herrick and Kinderberg stressed in 1984 the negative effects of inappropriate financial mechanism on economic development. They believed that the distorted and controlled finance mechanism would hinder the adjustments and reform of economic structure, thus blocking economic growth, which was referred to as the "financial blocking theory".

Therefore, inclusive finance is related to financial repression. With the development of inclusive finance, the phenomenon of financial repression can be eliminated, capital can flow through and market mechanism can freely play a role. Although financial repression can not be fundamentally removed in a short period, a sub-optimal result can be achieved, and the fundamental cause of financial repression can be overcome in the development process.

From the financial FSS indicators, cc represents the cost of capital.

cc= {inflation × (average total assets − average fixed assets)} + {(average total liabilities × market interest rates on debts) − actual financial costs}

It is clear that FSS and market interest rates on debts are in the opposite direction. Financial repression will result in the rise in market interest rates and the decline in corporate financial sustainability index. However, financial deepening will lead to the decline in market interest rates and thus will promote the improvement of financial FSS index as other conditions remain unchanged.

In terms of inclusive financial demand, financial deepening will naturally stimulate the demand for inclusive finance and encourage the inclusive financial demanders who are initially excluded from finance to participate in inclusive financial system, promoting the dynamic development of inclusive financial services.

In terms of financial infrastructure and services, after the financial deepening, the infrastructure and services will naturally follow up and relative standards will be established.

To conclude, the direct result of financial deepening is the reduction of market interest rates, and financial deepening will also have impact on the overall infrastructure and technology and improve the sustainability and balance of the overall financial system.

2.1.3.2 Dynamic Sustainability of Inclusive Financial Institutions: Risk

Identification and Avoidance

The index systems of WB[①] and IMF[②] measure the development level of inclusive finance from the demand side and the supply side respectively. The CGAP index system[③] combines demand-side and supply-side data, and the AFI[④] index system is characterized by the establishment of customized standards based on national conditions.

The dynamic sustainability of inclusive financial institutions lies in the matching of the risks and benefits during their operation. This issue is faced by any financial institution. Apart from this common issue, inclusive financial institutions also have different levels of vulnerability when facing risks as their interest rates are relatively high due to the characteristics of inclusive financial clients[⑤]. Therefore, to achieve dynamic sustainability, inclusive financial institutions should pay attention to risk identification and avoidance.

Main risk types include credit risk, market risk, operational risk, liquidity risk, legal risk, etc.

---

① As the World Bank (WB) index system mainly obtain data from the demand side, WB's indexes reflect the utilization of financial services. In addition, the WB index system covers relevant indicators of emergency funds such as the accessibility of related funds in emergencies and the sources of emergency funds (savings, friends and relatives, loans, etc.), which reflects whether financial development enhances people's ability to deal with risks to some extent.

② The IMF index system mainly reflects financial services on the supply side.

③ CGAP index system pays more attention to the role of financial service quality based on accessibility and utilization.

④ AFI index system also plans to include financial service quality into its index system in the future.

⑤ Asif Dowla. The Poor Always Pay Pack: The Garmeen II Story, 62.

Table 2.2 Risk Type and Risk Source in China

Risk Type	Risk Source
Credit risk	Demand side are unable to repay
Market risk	Interest rate fluctuations; other price fluctuations
Operational risk	Operational error
Liquidity risk	Term mismatch; liquidity problems
Legal risk	Illegal fund-raising; usury; money laundering; etc.

Source: www.shujn.wdzj.com

Therefore, the first characteristic of dynamic sustainability is the awareness and capability to identify and avoid risks so as to avoid the unsustainability of inclusive financial institutions due to any small problem.

In terms of the indicators in Chapter 5, identifying risks can effectively reduce loan loss reserves and operate income caused by changes in interest rates. Furthermore, operational risks and legal risks can be reduced through the enhancement of transparency so as to effectively increase the FSS numerical value.

2.1.3.3 Dynamic Sustainability of Inclusive Finance on the Demand Side: Financial Inclusion and Poverty Alleviation

In simple terms, the dynamic sustainability of inclusive finance on the demand side refers to the capability to maintain the demand for inclusive finance within a certain range in a dynamic system.

In the stage from dire poverty to relative poverty, demanders of inclusive finance still have certain financial needs. Therefore, to achieve the dynamic sustainability of inclusive finance on the demand side, it needs to be made sure that people will not fall into the stage of absolute poverty as a whole so as to sustain the demand.

Sustainability of inclusive finance is an interesting topic. The purpose of inclusive finance is to provide all financially excluded people with normal financial services. Therefore, inclusive finance objectively benefits the poor. However, if the number of the poor continues to decrease, then the original inclusive finance must be transformed, or inclusive finance cannot be sustained. Still, the poor always exist in the current social stage. Thus, this paper discusses the sustainability of inclusive finance in a self-consistent logical system and does not involve higher-level discussions[1].

In conclusion, the sustainability of inclusive finance on the demand side should be understood as serving a suitable number of people living in dire poverty, extreme poverty or moderate poverty, and as the poverty line is raised, inclusive financial demanders can still enjoy financial services compatible with the times, just like Rawls pointed out in *A Theory of Justice*, the bottom line of a society depends on the treatment the least well-off members of society receive. For example, the wealth and knowledge possessed by the poor nowadays may be what the rich had 100 years ago. The sustainability of inclusive finance on the demand side means that in situations where the social gap between the rich and the poor cannot be overcome, the poor can still have the needs for and access to sustainable financial services, such as basic bank accounts, insurance, basic wealth management, etc.

As poverty standards are raised, there has been no particularly large change in the relative population living in poverty. But there is no

---

[1] Jiao Jinpu. Building an Inclusive Financial System in China, 44.

doubt that even the poorest are already much better-off than what they were 30 years ago. For the sustainability of inclusive finance on the demand side, the existence of the relatively poor is the external source of the sustainability of inclusive finance.

2.1.3.4 Dynamic Sustainability of Inclusive Financial Systems: Dynamic Quantitative Management

Inclusive financial institutions seldom take into account the entire ecological balance in the development process. The entire inclusive financial system is only in a relatively supplementary position in macro finance. Based on the statistical analysis of CBRC in 2017[1], inclusive finance accounts for only 24% of the total lending volume in the financial industry. Still, inclusive finance and small and micro enterprise financing is still subject to monetary policies and quantitative regulation[2], which can be directly reflected in the cost of financing and the overall scale of inclusive finance.

The government has provided some support to inclusive finance in monetary and fiscal policies. When adjusting reserves and interest rates in the past few years, the government took full consideration of agriculture-related loans and inclusive finance. However, in the market environment, due to the existence of undifferentiated arbitrage, interest rates and the overall scale of financing still have a direct impact on inclusive finance. According to Chen Xin's research, the changes in interest rates brought about by monetary policies will directly affect the level

---

① According to the data from CBRC, total social financing in 2017 reached 273.3 trillion yuan.

② Chen Xin. Small and Micro Enterprise Financing and Monetary Policy Selection[J]. China's Economic Issues, 2017(6).

of profits and the sustainability of inclusive finance.

2.2 Inclusive Finance System Framework

2.2.1 Providers of Inclusive Finance

There are four main providers of inclusive financial services: banking financial organizations, non-banking financial organizations, non-governmental organizations and cooperative financial institutions. Some organizations only provide certain types of inclusive financial services and thus can not be regarded purely as inclusive financial institutions, Inclusive financial institutions including cooperative financial institutions, microcredit companies and emerging Internet financial institutions, provide more comprehensive and specific inclusive financial services.

Table 2.3 Main Providers in Inclusive Financial System

Name	Banking financial organizations	Non-banking financial organizations	Non-governmental organizations	Cooperative financial institutions
Type	State-owned commercial banks, postal savings banks, specialized microcredit banks, rural banks.	More than 200 kinds of organizations such as mortgage loan organizations, consumer credit associations, insurance companies, etc.	Professional non-governmental credit, cooperatives.	Cooperative organizations, credit unions.

Source: www.cbrc.gov.cn

Factors influencing the sustainability of inclusive financial providers are as follows:

(1)Sustainable profits

The reason why the concept of inclusive finance has attracted so much attention is that in traditional view, serving low-income groups can not bring about the expected profits compared with other financial services. This is also the main reason that low-income groups are excluded from traditional financial institutions.

(2)High cost of micro transactions

The clients of inclusive finance are mostly small business owners with small transaction amount and higher transaction frequency, which will create relatively high operating costs for inclusive finance providers. Therefore, the high cost of micro transactions should be carefully considered when determining the sustainability of inclusive finance.

(3)Pricing of financial products

The pricing power of inclusive financial products refers to the autonomy of inclusive financial institutions to determine the prices of their own financial products. Due to the public welfare nature and government regulation, many institutions that provide inclusive financial serves are not able to obtain enough revenues from their clients to cover the costs, and at the same time the support, financial subsidies and tax preference provided by government are short term. Therefore, considering the external support, the price of financial products must be able to cover the cost so as to achieve sustainable development and increase coverage[1], which requires inclusive financial institutions to have the pri-

---

[1] Jiao Jinpu. Building China's Inclusive Financial System[M]. China Financial Publishing House, 86.

cing power in varying conditions.

(4)Product diversification

From the perspective of a single inclusive financial institution, a-chieving scale management will help realize the sustainability of the institution, as fixed costs can be apportioned and the costs of a single transaction can be reduced. In order to achieve economies of scale, inclusive financial institutions can expand client coverage, establish customer stickiness, conduct repeated transactions, and expand business in highly populated areas in the initial stage. It is common for inclusive financial institutions to adopt a flat and horizontal approach: providing one or a few standard products to maintain lower labor, management and R&D costs. But in this way, the sustainable development of inclusive financial institutions can not be guaranteed in sparsely populated or highly competitive areas.

In contrast, a diversified and vertical product strategy will offer diversified financial products and services to clients and thus increase the business volume in all-inclusive financial branches and networks, helping achieve profitability and promote the sustainability of the institutions, especially in this Internet era. According to Gonzalez, about one-third of the sustainable microcredit institutions are able to cover their operating costs only when they receive revenues from multiple product at the same time.[1]

(5)Institutional alliances

Seen from the system of inclusive finance, an important connotation of inclusive finance is the organic integration of retail financial insti-

---

[1]   Adrian Gonzalez. Sources of Revenue and Assets Allocation at MFIs[J]. Micro Banking Bulletin, 2008.

tutions. Product diversification is of great significance for the sustainability of the institutions. However, it is unrealistic and uneconomical for a single institution to realize diversification in its entire product lines. As for inclusive finance clients, they only need to obtain financial services instead of knowing the entire internal process of financial services. Therefore, institutional alliances can not only enable institutions to break their individual limits and provide clients with package services but also expand opportunities and client coverage of the institutions and help them work jointly to resist risks and strengthen the advantages of internal labor division.

2.2.2 Demanders of Inclusive Finance

One misunderstanding in the research on the sustainability of inclusive finance is that the demand for inclusive finance is infinite, and that the sustainability of inclusive finance will be achieved as long as the Say's law is followed and high-quality inclusive financial services are provided. The problem here is that little stress is laid on the demand side of inclusive finance, which can be said as a prejudice violating the nature of inclusive finance. Equal attention should be given to the financial needs of the demand side and of other financial entities. Ignoring the needs of inclusive financial entities or valuing their needs only in some stage will hinder the sustainable development of inclusive finance.[①]

---

① In the initial stage, the demand for inclusive finance is relatively obvious and clear, but many inclusive financial institutions have the arrogance of welfarism, which is especially evident in relatively underdeveloped bureaucratic countries.

Table 2.4 Target Clients of Inclusive Finance

Target clients		Individuals in dire poverty
of inclusive	Target clients of mi-	Individuals in extreme poverty
finance	cro finance	Individuals in moderate poverty
		Economically vulnerable
		Non-impoverished individuals
		Well-off individuals

Source: Access to All (CGAP) page 20

2.2.3 Operational Efficiency of Inclusive Financial System

After analyzing the providers and demanders of inclusive finance, a simple inclusive financial system is formed. With no other disturbing factors, inclusive financial system can continue to operate as long as the providers provide financial services to the demanders, and the demanders pay corresponding prices to the providers.

Operating expenditures are needed for information seeking and transfer to reduce information asymmetry and to provide inclusive financial services to those who really need it. One actual challenge is that due to client characteristics[1], the adverse selection and moral hazard problem in inclusive financial system are more serious than that in normal financial system, which has increased the transaction costs on both sides and greatly reduced the operational efficiency of inclusive financial system, and even made the system unable to function effectively.

---

[1] Industry Development Report on China's Microcredit Companies (2005—2016), 24.

Tragedy of the Commons is manifested in the fact that fierce market competition has made inclusive financial institutions loosen their loan conditions at the outset without full grasp of the borrowers' specific purpose and ability to repay loans, resulting in over-indebtedness of the borrowers and systematic risk which will affect operational efficiency[1]. CSFI pointed out that over-indebtedness is the biggest problem faced by global microcredit industry[2]. Hence, it is essential for inclusive financial institutions to find lenders with good solvency.

2.2.4 Financial Infrastructure and Service Quality

Financial infrastructure mainly refers to the payment system and clearing system that guarantee the fast barrier-free payment among financial institutions and thus facilitate fast, accurate and safe capital transactions. Thus, to achieve the goal of inclusive finance, it is necessary and essential to have the financial infrastructure that can provide the payment system and clearing system with wide coverage, security, efficiency and reliability[3].

In most countries, commercial banks generally have relatively complete financial infrastructure. However, these financial institutions usually do not provide financial services to the poor in their well-established branch networks; instead, they often try to gain profits by meeting the demand of the poor at the lowest cost through cost-reducing service channels, of which the "direct banking services" such as Internet banking, mobile banking and ATMs in some microcredit institu-

---

① Industry Development Report on China's Microcredit Companies (2005-2016), 43

② Global Microcredit Finance Banana Skins 2015, CSFI.

③ Jiao Jinpu. Building China's Inclusive Financial System[M]. China Financial Publishing House, 113.

tions and developed countries are representative.

The application of new technology in financial infrastructure can bring late-mover advantages and enable more poor people to get financial services. Specifically, financial infrastructure is embodied in four aspects: (a) financial payment system; (b) information management system; (c) technical support system; (d) network support system. Only by coordinating and unifying the four systems can the completeness of the financial infrastructure be ensured. Otherwise, the wooden barrel effect and the single point of failure will be triggered and endanger the sustainability of inclusive finance[1].

2.2.5 Policies and Systems

Inclusiveness is an ideal state, but there is no such standard model for it. In practice, government promotion is needed to bring a variety of financial services through multiple channels to clients who are currently excluded by the traditional financial service system. This will fill the real gap between supply and demand, integrate scattered institutions serving the poor and assimilate the marginalized poverty alleviation financing systems into the country's financial strategy in order to maximize the potential of microfinance. Policies and systems in this process play a crucial role in the sustainability of inclusive finance.

---

[1] Xie Yumei. Comparative Study on the Development of Microcredit, 23.

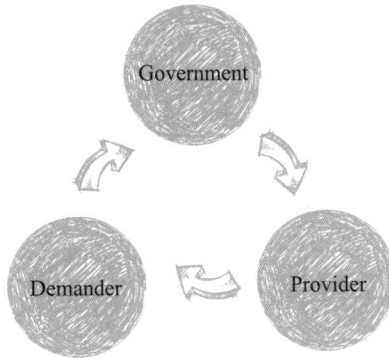

Figure 2.1 Main Parties in Inclusive Finance

The role of government in the establishment and sustainability of inclusive finance is mainly reflected in two aspects: first, to provide a sound and sustainable policy environment; second, to effectively regulate inclusive finance when it is included in the overall national financial system.

Based on the 2002 Monterrey Consensus[①], a sustainable policy environment requires:

(a) fair growth;

(b) macroeconomic stability;

(c) sound institutions;

(d) healthy financial systems;

(e) protection of the public;

(f) transparency and a competitive and fair-trading environment;

(g) positive reform driven by political economy.

The underlying issues of inclusive finance are essentially political and economic issues. The government's motivation of changes in mac-

---

① The Monterrey Consensus was the outcome of the 2002 Monterrey Conference, the United Nations International Conference on Financing for Development in Monterrey, Mexico. It was adopted by Heads of State and Government on 22 March, 2002.

ro-environment, in fact, will fundamentally promote the inclusiveness of inclusive finance.

State's effective regulation of inclusive finance can effectively correct market failures. Therefore, improving the regulatory system at the legal level, establishing regulatory principles and framework, and standardizing the means of supervision can help ensure the healthy and sustainable development of inclusive finance.

2.3 Indicator System of Inclusive Finance

2.3.1 Efficiency Indicator: Interest Rates and Interest Rate Control

One of the main features of inclusive finance is the relatively high interest rates for small loans. The control over high interest rates will affect the efficiency of the entire inclusive financial system. Meanwhile, excessively high interest rates will also hinder the further development of inclusive finance. Therefore, interest rates are an important indicator to judge whether the inclusive financial system is functioning effectively. In this respect, all countries have loosen their policies over inclusive finance compared with other financial sectors, but some countries also have the cap control. Still, a country's interest rate control should be placed in the specific economic and social environment instead of being judged simply based on the value.

In 2017, the Chinese government announced that personal lending rates should not exceed 36% [1]. Its purpose is to protect the inclusive fi-

---

① Announcement of CBRC, December 1, 2017.

nancial borrowers from high interest rates. As the price signal in the financial market, the interest rates play an important role in regulating the supply and demand. Once the interest rates are regulated, there will inevitably be some cases where the financial demand cannot be met, thus affecting the allocation efficiency.

R (annual effective interest rates) of the MFI is determined by five variables, each expressed as the percentage of the average loan balance: [1] AE (administrative expenditure ratio), LL (loan loss ratio), CF (capital cost ratio), K (expected capitalization ratio) and II (return on investment ratio).

$$R=(AE+LL+CF+K-II)/(1-LL)$$

Considering the objective existence of high LL and high CF that matches the high risks, interest rate control will inevitably lead to the failure of inclusive financial institutions to cover their effective costs and the inability of inclusive financial institutions to sustain. Therefore, for different inclusive financial institutions, their sustainability lies in whether $R < R*$ (regulated interest rates). If $R < R*$, inclusive financial institutions can enjoy long-term sustainability; if not, they will be unable to sustain.

Take the statistics on P2P001.com on October 17, 2017 as an example[2]. II=8.77%, AE=4.3% LL=9.2%, CF=13.1%, K=6.3%, R =26.45%, R* =36%. In this situation, most internet lending institutions were able to sustain.

However, in the above case, if the average interest rates in some institutions were higher than R* due to mismanagement or other rea-

---

[1]   CGAP, Micro Interest Rate, Occasional Paper NO 1, 2002.
[2]   http://www.p2p001.com/Yuqing/index.html

sons, then these institution's sustainability would face the direct threat of interest rate control in addition to business risks[1].

2.3.2 Financial Facilities and Services Quality: Indicator of Fair Access

The inclusive financial system includes not only the demanders and providers of financial services, as financial institutions can not survive and develop in a vacuum. Instead, the inclusive financial system relies on solid, well-functioning financial infrastructure and other service providers as well as information systems to promote the transparency in financial institutions, provide training and advisory services, and establish business associations and networks.

2.3.2.1 Transparency: An Important Indicator of Fairness

Financial transparency refers to the accurate, timely and comparable information available to market participants in relation to the performance of financial institutions. Transparency is the foundation for building an inclusive financial system. First, transparency can improve the performance of financial institutions. Correct information can not only help management identify areas to be improved and make better decisions, but also motivate the institution to improve performance through peer comparison. Second, transparency can attract more investors. Accurate, standardized information can encourage private investors or public donors to make better investment decisions, and the investment flow can lead to a rapid increase in the number of institutions

---

① Jiao Jinpu. Building China's Inclusive Financial System[M]. China Financial Publishing House, 159.

providing financial services to the poor. Third, transparency allows customers to compare and choose between different financial institutions, thus intensifying the competition among financial service providers. And this kind of competition driven by clients' free choice through open information will encourage financial institutions to offer better prices and services to attract clients. In addition, financial institutions with good transparency will find it easier to gain the trust of clients, especially the depositors.

Transparency includes a wide range of activities, entities and tools from product and report verification to the publication and utilization of information. The transparency of financial institutions depends on the good functioning of several steps that are related to and different from each other.

On October 28, 2016, China Internet Finance Association officially released the Standard for Internet Financial Information of Individual Internet Loans Disclosure (T/NIFA 1-2016) (hereinafter referred to as The Standard)[①]. The Standard defines and standardizes 96 indicators for information disclosure, including 65 mandatory disclosure indicators and 31 encouraging disclosure indicators, and determines the level of an institution's transparency based on the disclosure of the basic information, governance information, website or platform information, financial and accounting information, major issue information, platform operation information and project information.

2.3.2.2 Management and Utilization of Information

Management Information System (MIS) helps financial institutions

---

① http://www.sohu.com/a/117665848_479749

collect and disclose accurate and useful data in a timely manner. MIS is the cornerstone of financial transparency, and the quality of information at this stage affects all other dimensions. Internal controls and external audits help verify the quality, completeness and accuracy of the information provided by financial institutions. The performance evaluation is mainly to allow management and external participants, such as banking regulators, investors or clients, to monitor the performance of financial institutions over a period of time.

Benchmarking is a process in which a company compares its products and methods with those of other companies in its field, in order to try to improve its own performance. Benchmarking allows management and other stakeholders to know which level the institution is at compared with other financial institutions in the same field. Performance standards are the absolute standards financial institutions should follow.

Rating refers to the independent assessment of the credit or risks of financial institutions based on standardized methodologies. Regulators and investors can use the transparent financial information to determine the degree of risks in the financial institution and the entire financial system.

2.3.2.3 Technical Support Services

Technical support services, skill training and financial capacity building are the most needed meso-level services in the entire financial system. The development of the financial institution depends on the specialized training and counseling services to its employees provided by technical service providers, which cover financial management, business planning, training of employee expertise, market research, risk management, new product development, information technology solutions, employee incentive systems and human resource management systems. With the complexity of the financial system and the continuous improvement of network technology, financial institutions in many developing countries and remote areas have difficulty in keeping up with the pace of international financial development due to the lack of corresponding technical support services.

Technical support is a meso-level indicator, often using a rating system to evaluate the technical support in a particular region or field.

2.3.2.4 Business Associations and Networks

Over the past few decades, international, regional and national associations and networks in the financial sector have emerged. "Networks" usually refer to organizations that serve the financial institutions at the global or regional level, whereas "associations" are usually national (also some regional or global) organizations based on membership. These associations and networks have made an important contribution at the meso-level. They not only serve their members directly or indirectly, but also provide a channel for the collective voice of financial service providers. The main services include: policy advocacy, information publicity, capacity building, performance monitoring and financial intermediaries, etc. With the introduction of the concept of inclusive finance, various financial associations and networks are also paying increasing attention to social responsibility. Better serving the poor and clients in remote areas has become an important part of their work.

2.3.2.5 Financial Infrastructure

Bossone, an economist at WB, pointed out in his research that the construction of financial infrastructure was interlinked with the economic development, technological progress and changes in the financial systems in a country. Improving financial infrastructure could promote large-scale and efficient industrial capital accumulation. And the more developed the financial infrastructure is, the stronger its tolerance of external impact will be. The inclusive financial infrastructure is at the meso level of inclusive finance, integrating the features and nature of inclusive financial development with financial infrastructure. The inclusive financial infrastructure allows funds to flow among financial institutions, thereby facilitating fast, accurate and secure payment and clearing system. It covers the financial legal system, credit rating system, financial regulatory system, payment and settlement system, financial accounting and information system and the application of new technologies.

Financial infrastructure refers to the various hardware and software facilities for financial operation, which is the material basis and technical condition for the sustainable development of finance. It mainly covers the financial legal system, payment and settlement system, credit system and regulatory system, etc.

The development of financial infrastructure is of great significance to promote the development of financial markets, close the links between financial markets, speed up social capital turnover, improve the efficiency of resource allocation, prevent financial risks, promote the innovation of financial instruments and improve financial services. The construction of financial infrastructure is closely related to the stability of financial development, and the two are mutually reinforcing each other. Continuously strengthening the construction of financial infrastructure will lead to the corresponding development in money market, capital market, bill market, insurance market, foreign exchange market, gold market, etc. In this case, the financial function, the modern payment and settlement system will be more complete, and the level of financial services will steadily improve. Financial infrastructure construction is crucial for the financial stability of emerging and transition economies, which is the basic condition for financial stability. The role of financial infrastructure should not be underestimated.

The soundness of financial infrastructure is closely related to the development of financial innovation. Sound financial infrastructure helps to reduce the cost of investor information collection under information asymmetry to ensure the efficiency of the financial market to enhance the confidence of all parties in the financial market. Strong financial infrastructure provides guarantee and conditions for the development of financial innovation.

It should be noticed that different financial developments require different matching financial infrastructure. For example, if a country's financial system is fragile, its financial infrastructure is not complete and its experience in microfinance is poor, it will be premature for this country to establish credit bureaus and invest in sophisticated technology. In a more mature or larger market, on the other hand, a large number of competitive financial infrastructure services are needed to support the development of the financial system, such as electronic payment infrastructure, consultancy services, information and sale terminals and technical support. However, the fact is that payment systems in many countries fail to meet the needs of low-income clients to transfer funds nationwide in a safe, cost-effective and efficient manner. Some countries may make technological leaps and directly set up advanced electronic payment system, which will help to provide potentially more payment services to a large number of residents in the future to solve the above-mentioned problems.

With the continuous and comprehensive development of the financial industry in various countries in the world, different financial markets also put forward different requirements on the construction of financial infrastructure. Taking the development of inclusive finance as an example, inclusive financial associations and networks can improve the transparency of institutions' performance, develop new technology, enhance management skills, negotiate with service providers and investors and advocate policy changes through the collective strength of financial institutions and make micro financial transactions possible. Besides, inclusive financial infrastructure includes a wide range of participants.

However, at present, in most developing countries, large-scale promotion of financial services among the poor also requires better financial infrastructure and more relevant service providers, which requires not only marginalized specialized microfinance infrastructure and related service providers, but also mainstream financial infrastructure and related service providers to share this responsibility. Therefore, strengthening the construction of financial infrastructure plays an important role in financial development.

The construction of financial infrastructure needs to be compatible with the development of financial markets so as to promote the stable development of the financial industry. In return, the continuous development of finance has put higher requirements on the financial infrastructure. It can be said that financial infrastructure and financial development are complementary and interdependent.

Through the establishment of a modern inclusive financial development system, the integration of financial services from the developed cities to the underdeveloped urban areas and the more backward rural areas in China will be realized, which is of great significance to China's economic development and social construction. Many overseas scholars have carried out empirical research to prove the important relationship between economic development and financial support. Establishing an integrated and sustainable financial service system is an important part of the Twelfth Five-Year Plan, which will enable people of all walks of life to enjoy financial services conveniently.

To establish a sustainable and modern inclusive financial system, in addition to the government's effective support and supervision, the institutions themselves should pay more attention to the prevention of risks and actively expand the channels for operating capital so as to reduce their dependence on government support and poverty alleviation funds. In rural areas, the government should actively establish a rural capital inflow mechanism and an incentive and compensation mechanism for the inflow of rural funds to minimize the outflow of rural capital. Besides, in order to realize the sustainable development of modern inclusive finance, full attention should be paid to the control over credit risk of the inclusive financial demanders, to the improvement of the early warning ability of risks and to the reduction of bad loan ratio. As inclusive financial clients are mainly poor people with low income, low education level and poor credit concept, financial institutions that provide financial services to such groups should fully understand the actual production, living situation and credit information of these clients. Together with the financial institutions, the government should provide a sharing credit rating system for farmers, establish a credit information system and strengthen the risk control and identification capabilities of the business staff. In addition, the government should strengthen the cooperation with insurance agencies and other agencies to spread the risks and enhance institutions' risk tolerance.

2.3.3 Policies and Systems: Indicators of Competitiveness

The World Economic Forum, as one of the most famous institutions in the world for competitiveness evaluation, has evaluated the competitiveness of each country since 1979. The Global Competitiveness Report is an annual report that tracks the performance of close to 140 countries. It assesses the factors identified by empirical and theoretical research as determining improvements in productivity, which in turn is the main determinant of sustainable growth and an essential factor in economic growth and productivity. The GCI[①] (Global Competitiveness Index) is "a collection of policies, systems and influencing factors that determine the level of productivity in a country."

GCI is based on 12 pillars of competitiveness and fully reflects the competitiveness of countries in the world. The scores of the competitiveness index are the total scores of these indicators. The 12 pillars include institutions, infrastructure, macroeconomic environment, health and primary education, higher education and training, goods market efficiency, labor market efficiency, financial market development, technological readiness, market size, business sophistication and innovation. These 12 indicators correspond to the three stages of national economic development. Among them, indicator 1 to 4 are basic require-

---

① The Global Competitiveness Report 2016—2017

ments. Indicators 5 to 10 are efficiency enhancers. Indicators 11 to 12 are innovation and sophisticated factors.

According to the Global Competitiveness Report 2016—2017，China's global competitiveness has rapidly developed to a relatively advanced level.

Table 2.5 2012—2017 China's Rank and Value of GCI

	Rank	Scores
GCI 2016—2017	28/138	5.0
GCI 2015—2016	28/140	4.9
GCI 2014—2015	28/144	4.9
GCI 2013—2014	29/148	4.8
GCI 2012—2013	29/144	4.8
Subindex A: Basic requirements(1~7, 40%)	30	5.3
1. Institutions	45	4.3
2. Infrastructure	42	4.7
3. Macroeconomic environment	8	6.2
4. Health and primary education	41	6.2
Subindex B: Efficiency enhancers(1~7, 50%)	30	4.8
5. Higher education and training	54	4.6
6. Goods market efficiency	56	4.4
7. Labor market efficiency	39	4.5
8. Financial market development	56	4.2
9. Technology	74	4.0
10. Market size	1	7.0
Subindex C: Innovation and sophisticated factors (1~7, 10%)	29	4.2

Continued

	Rank	Scores
Business sophistication	34	4.4
Innovation	30	4.0

Source: Global Competitiveness Report 2016—2017

Global Competitiveness Report 2016—2017 covered a total of 138 economies in the world. The data were from the global surveys conducted by the UN, the WB, the IMF and the World Economic Forum. The report showed that the top 10 were still dominated by developed western economies and the four Asian Tigers, which ranked as follows: Switzerland (1st), Singapore (2nd), the United States (3rd), the Netherlands (4th), Germany (5th), Sweden (6th), Britain (7th), Japan (8th), Hong Kong (9th) and Finland (10th).

The overall competitiveness of Asian economies is improving. Singapore was second only to Switzerland in the world and Japan and Hong Kong ranked among the top 10. China, the most competitive economy among the major emerging markets, ranked 28th in the world, which is the same as the previous year, and took the leading role in BRIC countries. India rose to the 39th place. The top five ASEAN countries all ranked in the top half of the list, which were Malaysia (25th), Thailand (34th), Indonesia (37th), Philippines (47th) and Vietnam (56th).

2.4 Summary of the Framework of Inclusive Finance's Sustainability

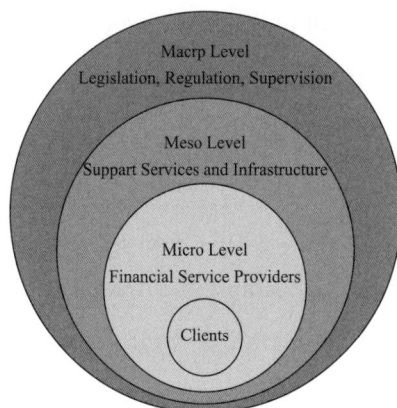

Figure 2.2 System of Inclusive Finance

Financial services of inclusive finance can be divided into three levels:

(a) the micro level, which provides retail financial services from private lending to commercial banking directly to the poor and low-income groups;

(b) the meso level, which deals with financial infrastructure and support services such as rating agencies, industry associations, professional business networks, settlement payment systems, credit bureaus, IT and technical advisory services that help providers realize lower transaction costs, expand service scope and enhance financial support and transparency;

(c) the macro level, which refers to the preferential regulations and policy frameworks of inclusive finance. The participants of this level only include the central bank, the Ministry of Finance and other related government agencies. In short, financial infrastructure refers to a set of regulations, legislation and supervision that supports the effective functioning of financial markets and financial intermediaries. An important function of financial infrastructure is to effectively guide the transfer of savings to productive capital and allocate it to industries with maximized profits, which will eventually promote economic growth.

To summarize, the sustainability of inclusive finance depends primarily on the sustainability of providers, demanders, financial operating systems, financial infrastructure and government management and regulation. Deficiency on any side will hinder the realization of inclusive finance's sustainability. The role of welfare indicators and social governance performance in measuring the sustainability of inclusive finance may be subordinate or weakened.

Chapter 3　A General Introduction to the Inclusive Finance in China

3.1 Developmental Situation of Inclusive Finance in China

China's inclusive finance started since the introduction of the microcredit model of the Grameen Bank in Bangladesh in 1994[①]. Taking the start-up of the "Credit-only" pilot project in 2005 as the standardization of inclusive finance in China, China's microcredit can be divided into three stages. The first stage (1994—1999) was the poverty alleviation stage dominated by NGOs. In the second stage (2000—2004), rural credit cooperatives became the main force. The third stage (2005—the present) witnessed the trend of formalization and commercialization of microcredit.

Specifically, if considering the services, types of financial products, targets of financial services, differences in development concepts and the breadth and depth of the platform, the development of inclusive finance in China could be divided into four stages.

(1)Nonprofit microcredit stage

In the early 1990s, China began to develop microcredit, whose main purpose was to alleviate poverty and serve the public. In 1993, the

---

① Lin Hanchuan. 2011 Research Report on the Development of Small and Medium Sized Enterprises[M]. Enterprise Management Publishing, 2011.

first microcredit institution in China, the Poverty Alleviation Economic Cooperation, was established in Yixian County, Hebei Province to improve the social status and economic conditions of poor farmers. In 1994, the Seven-year Priority Poverty Reduction Program (1994—2000) issued by the State Council indicated that the state used public welfare microcredit as a tool to solve the problem of rural poverty. Since 1996, the state has successively formulated relevant policies to promote the development of microcredit.

In June 1999, after the Central Conference on Poverty Alleviation and Development[①], the nonprofit microcredit was strongly advanced. Funding in this stage mainly came from soft loans or the donation of individuals or international agencies, aiming to improve the poverty situation in rural areas.

(2) Expansible microfinance stage

At the end of the 20th century, a well-off society was basically built in China. People's demand for financial services could not be satisfied through the original nonprofit microcredit model. China's finance developed into the expansible microfinance stage as people needed more specific and diversified financial services. Therefore, the People's Bank of China proposed setting up a loan file for rural households and providing them with loans based on their own credit without mortgage or guarantee. In this stage, microcredit was transformed from the main poverty alleviation tool into a tool to raise the income of farmers and promote employment rate, and no longer had the nature of public wel-

---

① The Central Conference on Poverty Alleviation and Development was held by the Central Committee of the Chinese Communist Party and the State Council in Beijing from June 8 to June 9, 1999. State Councilor and Secretary-General of the State Council Wang Zhongyu presided over the meeting.

fare. Participants included formal financial institutions, NGOs and semi-government organizations, and the scale of microcredit system expanded.

(3)Comprehensive inclusive finance stage

In 2005, China entered the stage of comprehensive inclusive finance. In the following years, the number and size of microcredit organizations has been continuing to grow. In December 2016, the number of microcredit institutions in China reached 8663, the number of employees was 108881 and the loan balance of small-sized companies was up to 9272.8 billion[1]. Many banking financial institutions innovated financial products and services, providing services to small and micro clients, such as settlement, online banking, payment, mobile banking, remittance, etc. In March 2007, Sichuan Yilong Huimin Rural Bank, China's first rural bank, was opened. In June 2009, the "Interim Provisions on the Structural Reform of Microcredit Companies and the Establishment of Community Banks" released by CBRC stipulated specific conditions for the restructuring of microcredit companies into community banks. Community banks played a more important role in addressing "the issues of agriculture, farmer and rural area" and supporting microcredit and became a core part in the reform of rural financial institutions. The inclusive financial services at this time not only included comprehensive financial services such as payment, remittance, loans and pawn, but also showed the trend of network and mobile services.

(4)Innovative internet finance stage

Up to December 31, 2014, the number of internet users in China was 649 million, ranking the first in the world, and the number of mo-

---

① http://www.sohu.com/a/125815849_351022

bile internet users reached 557 million. With the emergence of new internet products like YueBao and Alipay, a great variety of financial services such as Internet payment, Internet lending and online investment could all be accessed via the Internet. During this period, the rapid development of Internet finance formed three major trends: (1) using third-party payment and mobile payment instead of traditional payment; (2) using P2P credit instead of traditional deposit-loan business; (3) using crowdfunding instead of traditional securities business. The inclusiveness of inclusive finance payment in China took the lead in the world.

With Internet technology as the core, institutions represented by emerging companies are exploring new paths and driving changes in inclusive financial practice through the use of emerging technologies. With big data, cloud computing, and knowledge mapping technologies, China's inclusive finance has realized comprehensive improvements in credit management, risk control, product design and customer experience, and enhanced the inclusiveness of inclusive finance by providing more diversified financial products and services. In this process, the breadth and depth of the coverage of inclusive finance have been further expanded. These explorations and practices have provided integrated financial services for a wider range of people and businesses, which are realized through the combination of the later-mover advantages of China's inclusive finance and modern technology. In this way, the inclusive finance in China effectively overcomes problems like information asymmetry and high transaction costs that traditional inclusive finance may face, and provides the groups who were once excluded from financial system with adequate services. This should be a normal result of the development of financial service technology. However, the regions and countries with traditionally developed finance like Singapore are not able to obtain the later-mover technological advantages as China does due to the existence of sunk costs, depreciation and updating. Besides, they do not have the scale effects as China do, as China enjoys a wide range of groups with diversified inclusive financial needs. It should be noticed that the Chinese government has also played a significant role in promoting the development of inclusive finance in China.

Inclusive financial infrastructures and services include networks and technical support, and the most important indicators are credit investigation coverage and payment coverage, which could reflect the development of the credit investigation services and payment services of the inclusive financial system respectively.

The development of inclusive finance in the 21th century is based not on more bank branches but on the basic software infrastructure, namely, the payment coverage and the credit coverage. In 2016, the credit investigation coverage of inclusive finance in China was 35%, and the payment coverage of inclusive finance in China was 98.32%[1], indicating that China's inclusive finance has high payment coverage, but its credit investigation coverage needs to be further developed.

In short, although inclusive finance in China started relatively late, its development is really fast, in which both government guidance and regulation have played significant roles. However, there also exist a series of problems:

(1) the government intervention is not appropriate, which leads to obvious opposite effects, such as fettering its growth with too many policies and inhibiting the sustainable development of inclusive finance

---

[1] 2016 PBOC Payment System Development Report, 2016 PBOC Credit Center Report

with inappropriate interest rate regulation[1];

(2)laws and regulations are not sound, which leads the lack of a reasonable identity of inclusive financial institutions to engage in inclusive financial services and enjoy corresponding preferential policies, thus affecting their development. More importantly, the ambiguity on the supervision side and the lack of unified standards for the operation of inclusive financial institutions give rise to several problems;

(3)inclusive financial institutions lack of funds and other effective financing channels;

(4)the operation and management of inclusive financial institutions are inadequate.

3.2 Financial Sustainability of Providers of Inclusive Financial Services in China

The providers of inclusive financial services in China can be divided into the following four categories: banking financial institutions (including commercial banks, postal savings banks, specialized microcredit banks), non-bank financial institutions, (including loan companies, etc.), non-governmental organizations and cooperative financial institutions (see Table 2.3).

The emerging Internet finance companies use the Internet and P2P platforms to transfer the funds from those with surplus funds to those short of funds. In essence, they serve as financial intermediaries handling financial transactions. Still, Internet financial companies have the

---

[1]　Xie Yumei. Comparative Study of the Development of Microcredit[M]. Higher Education Press, 6.

nature of cooperative finance as what really works is the nature of mutual assistance between the providers and the demanders. In general, P2P can be classified as a non-bank financial organization.

Table 3.1 Statistical Analysis of Microcredit Institutions in China

	Number of institutions	Number of employees	Paid-up capital (100 million yuan)	Loan balance (100 million yuan)
end-March 2017	8643	108128	8271.4	9608.2
end-June 2017	8665	109078	8234.0	9377.3
end-June 2016	8810	115199	8379.2	9364.0
end of 2016	8673	108881	8233.9	9272.8
First half year growth number	−30	−753	37.5	335.4
First half year growth rate	−0.3%	−0.7%	0.46%	3.62%

Source: www.cbrc.gov.cn

From end-June 2016 to end-June 2017, there were 1931 Internet lending platforms, the turnover of P2P Internet lending industry was 224.809 billion yuan, and the loan balance was 437.221 billion yuan[1]. As to the end of December 2016, the total trading volume was 34.29093 trillion yuan; by the end of December 2017, the total trading volume of P2P Internet lending industry reached 6.233941 trillion yuan, an increase of 81.8% year on year.

---

[1] http://shuju.wdzj.com/industry—list.html

3.3 Financial Sustainability of Demanders of Inclusive Financial Services in China

The demand side of inclusive finance is an important part of the inclusive financial service system, and the sustainability of the demand side is also an important indicator of the sustainability of inclusive finance. For the inclusive financial system, the sustainability of the demand side is reflected in two aspects: the overall sustainability of the demand and the financial sustainability of the individual demander.

The financial sustainability of the individual demander refers to this individual's capability to cover his/her expenditures with income. Whereas the sustainability of the overall demand deals with the global issue of poverty, and is what this paper focused on. Poverty is one of the world's "Three P" issue (i.e. pollution, population, poverty). Governments over the world are all plagued by poverty. For example, both developing and developed countries are troubled with the slum issue in their urbanization or development process.

Eliminating poverty is an important issue in the UN Millennium Development Goals. The Chinese government has always attached great importance to the poverty problem, but in the face of a large number of the poor, continuous in-depth study and reasonable measures are required. Before the 1980s, poverty was generally understood from a material and economic point of view as the limited chances for certain people to eat, live and participate in certain activities. While the 1990 World Development Report defined poverty as lacking the ability to meet the minimum living standards such as health, education and nutrition. The report stated that measuring living standards should took into account not only household income and per capita expenditure, but also social welfare, such as health care, life expectancy, literacy level and access to public goods or common property resources, further expanding the concept of poverty by defining poverty as material scarcity, low-level education and health, as well as risks and vulnerabilities when facing risks.

The definition of poverty line by the National Bureau of Statistics of China is as follows: the poverty line, also called as poverty threshold, is the smallest amount of money a person or a family needs to live on under certain social conditions.

At present, China adopts the Martin Law[1] to determine the rural poverty line, which is a relatively advanced research method widely adopted in the world and suitable to China's national conditions.

The Martin Law can be broadly described as:

Absolute poverty line in rural China in a given period=Food poverty line + Non-food poverty line.

This method of identifying rural poverty line has the advantage of centralizing the most important part of people's basic needs of living—food consumption, while reasonably taking into account clothing, housing, transportation, fuel, supplies, healthcare, education, recreation, services and other consumption, and with simple operation, results of this method are very close to those of more complex methods.

Since 1993, Chinese cities have set their own poverty lines. Due to the different economic and social development levels of cities in China, it was difficult to formulate a unified national poverty line. In 2015, the

---

[1] The Martin Law is a method of poverty line calculation that was developed by Mr. Martin, an economist working for the World Bank.

Central Conference on Poverty Alleviation and Development announced that in accordance with the goal of building an overall well-off society by 2020 and in order to meet the situation that China's poverty alleviation and development had turned to a new stage, the central government decided to set the per capita net income of farmers at 1300 yuan as the new national poverty line, which was 92% higher than the standard of 1196 yuan in 2009. The number of people living below the poverty line by the end of 2011 was 128 million, accounting for about 13.4% of the rural population. The poverty line in China is consistent with the work orientation of "subsistence allowances to survive, poverty alleviation to promote development", and is basically the same with the self-determined poverty line in all provinces. Since the promulgation of the Outline of Poverty Alleviation and Development in Rural China 2011—2020, 29 provinces, autonomous regions and municipalities have put forward their views on the formulation of local poverty line. At present, the average of local poverty line in China's 31 provinces, autonomous regions and municipalities is about 2200 yuan .

With more than 30 years' rapidly economic growth, China has made remarkable achievements in anti-poverty work. Rural residents' living conditions have been greatly improved, the poverty situation has been alleviated significantly, and the number of the poor and the incidence of poverty have dropped sharply. The WB President Paul Wolfowitz mentioned in 2005 that since 1980, China's population out of poverty accounted for 75% of the out-poverty population in developing countries. China's anti-poverty achievements have been widely recognized by poverty researchers, international organizations and other poverty alleviation organizations at home and abroad.

With the great achievements in anti-poverty work, however, inclusive finance is facing this question: if poverty is eliminated, is there any need for inclusive finance to exist, or can the sustainability of inclusive finance be maintained? This paper argues that the demanders of inclusive finance are not only people in absolute poverty and related enterprises, but also people in the relative poverty, who are more important for the sustainability of inclusive finance and will always exist.

Therefore, the overall development of inclusive finance on the demand side is positively related to the sustainability of demand for inclusive finance. Although the number of people living in absolute poverty is decreasing, the percentage of people living in relative poverty with the rising poverty line has remained stable. For example, after the changes in poverty line, the poverty rate in 2008 and 2012 were both around 10%. Hence, the demand side of inclusive finance always exists.

$$Dif = apTs + c$$

c indicates fixed demand for inclusive finance. α indicates individual fixed financial demand ratio, P refers to the percentage of poor population, T refers to total population. S refers to poverty standard.

As can be seen from the above formula, the demand for inclusive finance depends on five variables, of which, c and α are often fixed values. It is P that have a major impact on the total demand for inclusive financial services.

3.4 External Driving Forces of Inclusive Financial Development in China

3.4.1 The United Nations

In 2005, the United Nations introduced the concept of inclusive finance and called for the building of inclusive financial systems. In 2006, the United Nations issued "Building Inclusive Financial Sectors" and proposed three key factors: (1) individuals, families, businesses and participants at all levels should be able to obtain appropriate financial services at reasonable prices, including credit, insurance, savings, wealth management, currency exchange and other services; (2) financial institutions should be well developed and properly supervised under appropriate industrial standards, access mechanisms, and internal controls; (3) inclusive financial institutions must be financially sustainable.

After UN proposed the year of inclusive finance and defined the rules for the construction of inclusive financial systems, inclusive finance in China and the entire world has been greatly promoted and a series of inclusive financial institutions have been established under the UN framework. The development of inclusive finance has been accelerated in accordance with the actual conditions of each country.

China's inclusive finance started relatively late and at the same time relied mainly on China's traditional financial system. For a considerable period of time, China's inclusive finance developed in a quite unique way. Then, with UN's promotion, informal financial forces, opportunities in market mechanism development and emerging Internet technologies, China's inclusive finance has developed rapidly.

3.4.2 Financial Reform after the American Financial Crisis

In 2008, affected by the U.S. sub-prime crisis, Occupy Wall Street movement began in New York city. The traditional American model in which large companies and enterprises were the vested interest groups was questioned and challenged. Especially, Citibank had its stock price plummeted and it suffered such heavy losses that it had to rely on special loans from the U.S. Department of the Treasury to survive. Compared with Citibank, other community banks suffered relatively little by the subprime crisis, and they recovered in a shorter time. After the subprime crisis, the United States has carried out a series of reforms to the traditional financial system and placed more emphasis on the supervision of traditional financial models. Community banks have received favorable policies and obtained good opportunities for development due to changes in market preferences, which has offered China valuable experience for reference.

3.4.3 Financial Fairness

Financial fairness and justice are the reflection of equal political consciousness and the embodiment of basic human rights in the financial field. The concept of financial fairness is not only an outcome of social productivity at a certain stage, but also the fundamental demand in a civil society. In 2005, when the United Nations proposed the concept of inclusive finance, financial exclusion had already made about one billion people around the world fail to obtain appropriate and fair financial services, which was a key social issue. China, as a responsible country, has always been committed to the development of a fair social order, but for a long time, financial equity was not a major concern. When the concept of financial fairness was put forward, China's economy had already developed to a certain stage, and inclusive finance has provided a viable path to achieve China's financial fairness. Specifically, the financial industry has achieved fast-track development and financial fairness has received great attention.

3.4.4 Financial Globalization

The process of financial globalization is a process in which financial capital seeks opportunities for financial development on a global scale, expands financial channels, and provides more extensive and in-depth financial services. However, on the other hand, it is also a process in which non-profit or low-profit domestic demand is excluded by financial capital and financial services. Financial globalization is a double-edged sword. To a certain extent, it is the inherent demand of financial development itself. But for inclusive finance, it is more important to provide localized basic financial services. Financial globalization can bring scale and spillover effects to the entire financial system, and the internal allocation of financial resources may squeeze out the resources of inclusive finance and reduce the space for the development of inclusive finance. Therefore, financial globalization would make an impact on inclusive finance in the short term. Besides, financial globalization is part of the globalization of production and development; as long as other social development and reforms can go together with financial globalization, financial globalization will promote the development of inclusive finance to a certain extent.

For China, China's financial system has benefited from the impact of financial globalization, and has received some of the international financial resources, which has helped increase China's financial supply. But in the meantime, local companies in China have also been affected by financial globalization. Still, in general, inclusive finance has provided a new path for China's domestic financial services.

3.4.5 Disparity between the rich and the poor

There are many objective reasons for the existence of the gap between the rich and the poor, which has led to unequal opportunities, class solidification and serious social problems. In this regard, inclusive finance in China should play an important role in eliminating the gap between the rich and the poor and promoting fair opportunities. For every citizen, the resource within their household may not guarantee them fair opportunities, and inclusive finance should help eliminate this inequality to a certain extent, thus reducing the negative impact of the disparity between the rich and the poor.

3.5 Internal Driving Forces of Inclusive Financial Development in China

3.5.1 Impact of Technology

One of the most important internal driving forces in the development of inclusive finance is technology, especially the Internet technology. Conventional inclusive financial institutions will suddenly fall across the issue of sustainability even when they have no problem in payment or risk control in the traditional economy[1].

According to the Statistical Report on Internet Development in China, by December 2015, the number of Internet users in China reached 688 million, the Internet penetration hit 50.3%, and the number of mobile internet users was 620 million[2]. Internet and mobile internet have

---

[1]　Huang Guoping. Introduction and Assessment of China Internet Finance Industry [M]. Social Sciences Literature Publishing House, 2016,3.

[2]　http://www.cnnic.net.cn/gywm/xwzx/rdxw/2016/201601/t20160122_53283.htm

changed the form of social life and financial consumption. From the payment data, in 2015, electronic payment became widely accepted by the public. "Technology + Finance" has pushed financial services to break through the physical restrictions and make the services develop in the direction of large scale and mobility.

In the emerging field, Internet finance (ITFIN) is a new type of financial business model in which traditional financial institutions and Internet companies make use of Internet technologies, information and communication technologies to provide financing, payment, investment and information intermediary services. ITFIN is the integration of internet technology and financial functions, and refers to the functional financial form and its service system supported by big data and cloud computing, which includes the network platform based on financial market system, financial service system, financial organization system, financial product system and the Internet financial regulation system, etc. The financial models of ITFIN, such as inclusive finance, platform finance, information finance and fragmented finance, are different from traditional finance models.

The development patterns of ITFIN include:

(1)Crowdfunding[①].

Crowdfunding through the Internet platform lets artists or individuals show their ideas and projects to the public and gain the necessary financial assistance from who support their ideas or projects. Crowdfunding platforms operate in much the same way: individuals or teams who need funding hand over their projects to crowdfunding platforms, and after the projects are reviewed and approved, individuals or teams

---

① Crowdfunding is the practice of raising funds for a project by collecting money from a large number of people, typically via the Internet.

will be able to create their own interfaces on the platform to introduce the project to the public.

(2)P2P Lending

P2P (Peer-to-Peer lending) is the practice of lending money to individuals or businesses through third-party Internet platforms that match lenders with borrowers. Borrowers can find out the possible lenders who have the capacity and willingness to lend them money on certain conditions. P2P lending helps the lenders spread risks through the cooperation with other lenders who are willing to share the lending. P2P lending also helps borrowers find favorable interest rate terms with sufficient information[1].

(3)Third-party payment

Third-Party Payments in a narrow sense refers to a form of payment where an intermediary non-bank institution handles the payment between a user and bank payment and settlement systems through the use of communication technology, computer and information security technology under contract with major banks[2].

---

[1]   There are two operation models of P2P lending. The first is a purely online model, in which both lending and borrowing activities are carried out online with no offline auditing. Common measures to review the qualifications of borrowers include video authentication, examination of bank bills, identity authentication, etc. The second is a combination of online and offline model. After the borrower submits the loan application online, the platform reviews the borrower's credit and repayment capability through household surveys conducted by the agent in his city.

[2]   According to the definition of payment services of non-financial institutions in PBOC's 2010 Regulations for the Payment Services of Non-financial Institutions, third-party payment refers broadly to financial services such as online payment, prepaid cards, bank card receipts in which non-financial institutions serve as an intermediary and handles the payment between a purchaser and a vendor and other services proved by PBOC. Third-party payment is not limited to the original internet payment; it has become a payment tool with online and offline coverage and comprehensive application.

Table 3.2 Developing Situation of Some

Digital Inclusive Financial Institutions

Financial institutions	Number of institutions	Developing situation
Bank	224, 000 branches of banks (by the end of 2015)	By the end of June 2016, the balance of agriculture-related loans (excluding bill financing) of banking financial institutions reached 273000 yuan, a YOY growth of 8.7%; the balance of loans to small and micro enterprises was 250000 billion yuan, an increase of 13.2%; From January to June in 2016, the banks handled 21.47 billion online payment businesses with a total amount of 1131.88 trillion yuan; 101 million telephone payment services with an amount of 6.12 trillion yuan and 117.52 mobile payment transactions with an amount of 81.45 trillion yuan.
Third-party payment	267 (by October 2016)	From January to June in 2016, non-bank payment agencies handled 67.714 billion online payment transactions with an amount of 41.93 trillion yuan.
P2P lending platform	2202 (by September 2016)	By September 2016, P2P lending industry's turnover reached 2.776226 trillion yuan, and its loan balance increased to 7130.42 billion yuan.

Continued

Financial institutions	Number of institutions	Developing situation
Crowdfunding platform	415 (by September 2016)	In September 2016, a total of 6,445 projects were successfully launched in the crowdfunding industry, collecting a total of 1,289 million yuan, of which 1,023 million yuan was reward-based crowdfunding, 228 million was equity crowdfunding (17. 69% of the total crowdfunding), and 38 million yuan was donation-based crowdfunding.

Source: CBRC; People's Bank of China; Yingcan Consulting; WDZJ.com

(4)Digital currency

Apart from the thriving third-party payment, P2P lending, microcredit, crowdfunding and YueBao, the Internet currency represented by Bitcoin has also begun to enter the stage of inclusive finance.

On August 19, 2013, the German government officially recognized the legitimate status of bitcoin, which could then be used for tax purposes and other legitimate purposes. Germany is also the first country in the world to recognize bitcoin. The ultimate form of Internet finance is digital currency[①]. Internet finance at present only challenges the existing commercial banks and securities companies. The future development of the internet currency will be a challenge to the central bank.

(5)Big data finance

Big data finance refers to the collection of massive unstructured da-

---

① Yang Hongmei. Digital Technology Assists in the Development of Inclusive Finance [J]. China Business News, 2017.

ta. Through real-time analysis, big data finance can provide Internet financial institutions with comprehensive client information and targeted approaches in marketing and risk control through analyzing and digging for information about clients' transactions and consumption in soder to understand clients' consumption habits and accurately predict their behavior.

The big-data-based financial service platform mainly refers to the financial services carried out by e-commerce enterprises with massive data. The key to big data is the ability to quickly access useful information from a large amount of data or the ability to quickly liquidate from big data assets. The information processing of big data is often based on cloud computing.

(6)Internet informatized financial institutions

Informatized financial institutions refer to financial institutions such as banks, security companies and insurance companies that have realized e-management and e-operation by transforming or reconstructing the traditional operating procedures with information technology. Financial informatization is one of the trends in the financial industry, and the informatized financial institutions are the product of financial innovation.

(7)E-financial portals

5—financial portals refer to the platforms where financial products are sold or where third-party services are provided for the sale of financial products through the Internet. The core of e-financial portals is the search-for-comparison model, which adopts the method of vertical comparison of financial products' prices by placing the products of various financial institutions on the platforms and letting the users select the appropriate financial products through comparison[①].

3.5.2 Government Promotion

Over the past few years, banking service coverage has expanded and the financial infrastructure has been improved, which should be attributed to the government's implementation of new goals and new policies. After China established the goal of inclusive finance in 2008, the government has formulated preferential policies on inclusive financial infrastructure and construction. In particular, the new financial model based on Internet finance, a form of inclusive finance, has become an important force in inclusive finance. With the rise of Internet finance, the inclusive finance in China has technically solved the problems of asymmetric information and financial exclusion, and greatly reduced the transaction costs. In recent years, China's inclusive finance has been in the first rank in the world (see Table 3.3 below).

These achievements were made while China was in the process of the transformation of the urban-rural dual structure. Hence, the importance of promoting the process of urbanization should never be neglected while developing rural economy and inclusive finance. In brief, China need to rapidly develop urban inclusive finance and promote the transformation of inclusive finance in rural areas. To achieve this purpose, the economic basis needs to be changed for the existence of inclusive finance.

---

① Showing the trend of innovation and diversity, E-financial portals have formed third-party financial management institutions that provides high-end wealth management services and products as well as insurance portal websites that provide advice on insurance products, price comparison, and purchase of services. This model does not involve too many policy risks, because the platform is not responsible for the actual sale of financial products, and do not bear any adverse risks. Besides, the funds do not go through the intermediate platforms.

Table 3.3 2012 CGAP Comprehensive Ranking of
Inclusive Finance in the World

No.	Indicator	China's index	Ranking/total number of countries and regions with index	Countries or Regions Ranking the 1st in the World	Index of Countries or Regions Ranking the 1st in the World	Average of G20 countries
1	Disclosure index (including language conciseness and accuracy, use of local language, clear loan fees and other requirements) (1—5 points, up to 5 points)	5	1%	22 countries tied for the 1st	5	4.06
2	Index for Internal and External Dispute Resolution Mechanism (0 / 0.5 / 1, up to 1)	1	1%	76 countries tied for the 1st	1	0.94
3	Proportion of adults saving in formal financial institutions (women)	41.16%	17%	Norway	80.9%	33.62%
4	Proportion of adults saving in formal financial institutions	41.15%	18%	Norway	78.41%	35.45%
5	Proportion of adults saving in the formal financial institutions (income level in the top 60%)	48.40%	18%	Sweden	80.96%	41.88%

Continued

No.	Indicator	China's index	Ranking/total number of countries and regions with index	Countries or Regions Ranking the 1st in the World	Index of Countries or Regions Ranking the 1st in the World	Average of G20 countries
6	Proportion of the average cost per US $ 200 overseas remittance (higher ranking, higher remittance cost)	11.73%	19%	Malawi	27.49%	8.98%
7	Proportion of adults saving in financial institutions (income level in the bottom 40%)	30.51%	20%	Norway	74.96%	26.04%
8	Proportion of adults saving in formal financial institutions (men)	41.15%	20%	Norway	75.93%	37.25%
9	ATMs per 1,000 km²	55.75	22%	Macau, China	38607.15	62.98
10	Number of borrowers per 1,000 adults in commercial banks	293.86	27%	Singapore	1149.08	423.31
11	Proportion of adults holding accounts in formal financial institutions (income level of bottom 40%)	72.04%	29%	Denmark, Finland, Norway	100%	71.03%
12	Proportion of adults holding accounts in formal financial institutions	78.93%	30%	Denmark, Finland, Norway	100%	76.50%

Source: 2012 CGAP Inclusive Financial Report

3.6 Summary

Judging from the sustainability indicators of inclusive finance in China, first, most formal inclusive financial institutions with available information are financially sustainable. However, the problem is that many inclusive financial institutions in China are not formalized and do not have available financial statements or standardized management. Thus, this paper takes a cautiously optimistic attitude towards the sustainability of inclusive financial institutions. Second, seen from the demand side, the number of people in absolute poverty in China has greatly decreased while the number of people in relative poverty is still huge. Therefore, inclusive finance will not face the problem of insufficient demand for the foreseeable future. Third, an indicator of the efficiency of the inclusive financial system is interest rate control. Lower controlled interest rates will reduce the space for inclusive finance to develop and affect the efficiency of inclusive finance. The adequate interest rate control should follow the welfare nature of inclusive finance. Fourth, financial infrastructure and financial service quality have enjoyed rapid growth in the past few years. Fifth, government management and transparency have been enhanced compared with the previous years.

Chapter 4　Sustainability of Inclusive Finance in China

4.1 Special Background of the Sustainability of Inclusive Finance in China: Urban-rural Dual Structure

China's urban-rural dual structure is not only reflected in industry and agriculture, but also reflected in the urban and rural areas. Through China's financial development, rural finance has been lagging behind urban finance for a long time. In view of the financial market, the financial market in urban areas basically serves the urban economic entities and consists of the branches of modernized banks, which include state-owned commercial banks, other commercial banks and foreign-funded banks, and security and insurance business. Whereas in the rural areas, the financial market mainly consists of small-sized rural commercial banks, rural credit cooperatives and other informal financial institutions[1] and serves rural economic entities.

4.1.1 Urban-rural Dual Structure in China

As a large agricultural country with a huge population, China has

---

[1]　Xin Yao. Research on Rural Lending in Underdeveloped Areas[M]. Shanghai Sanlian Bookstore, 30.

formed a development model with urban and rural isolation based on the disparities between China's urban and rural areas and has developed a unique urban-rural dual economic structure in the process of industrialization, urbanization and modernization. An important phenomenon closely related to the urban-rural dual economic structure in China is that there is a huge difference in the financial development between urban and rural areas in China. This financial gap interacts with and reinforces the gap between urban and rural economic development.

The urban-rural dual financial structure has caused a serious of problems, such as the widening gap between the rich and the poor, unbalanced regional development, over-proportion of the rural population, low productivity of agriculture, slow growth of farmers' income and large surplus of agricultural labor force, which have seriously hindered the overall economic and social development.

Difficulty in increasing farmers' income at this stage reflects not only the profound changes in the internal and external environment of agriculture and rural areas, but also various underlying conflicts that have long been accumulated under urban-rural dual financial structure. The essence of coordinating urban and rural development is to change the dual financial structure of urban and rural areas and solve "the three issues of agriculture, rural areas and farmers". According to the theory of modern financial development, with the interaction between the financial sectors and the real economic sectors, poor countries often fall into the trap of financial repression and economic stagnation[1], and the lifting of financial repression will improve resource utilization efficiency

---

① Tian Bao. Study on the Financial Support for Rural Economic Development[M]. Lanzhou University Press, 39.

and promote the development of the entire national economy. Besides, developing countries should give priority to the development of the financial industry and can not let the finance lag behind the economic growth.

Therefore, an important way to solve the problems brought about by the urban-rural dual economic structure in China is to balance the financial development in urban and rural areas. The urban-rural dual financial structure actually reflects the long-existing urban-oriented development in China[1].

After 1949, under the pressure of the external environment (international economic politics) and the constrains of the internal conditions (economic and political resources), the Chinese government chose the strategy of giving priority to heavy industry to realize rapid modernization under the influence of the Soviet Union. However, at that time, there was a direct contradiction between the capital-intensive heavy industry and the capital shortage and low resource mobilization in China. In order to reduce the cost of heavy industry, the state completely excluded the role of the market mechanism and artificially distorted the prices of production factors and products so as to provide cheap labor, capital, raw materials and imported equipment and technology to the development of the heavy industry. Distorting the price mechanism then was only a necessary means for the state to control resources and promote industrialization; to achieve its ultimate goal, the state must ensure that: first, capital and labor input has sufficient possession of agricultural surplus; second, industrial products must enjoy large market

---

① Liu Mingguo. China's Industrialization Strategy in the 21st Century[J]. Research on the Development in Underdeveloped Areas Ⅲ.

demand.

4.1.2 Financial Embodiment of Urban-rural Dual Structure

In terms of financial system, in order to ensure the resources needed for economic growth with heavy industry as the core, the state introduced the state-owned monopolistic financial property rights to support the capital supply of urban state-owned enterprises. To effectively
mobilize the surplus of rural economic resources, this kind of policy-oriented finance with roots in economic development strategy extended to
rural areas, obligating rural finance to submit to the planned economic
system and economic development strategy and to pipe the rural economic resources and surplus into industry and urban areas under state
control.

Through its control of rural economic resources and surplus, the
state has provided a large amount of primitive accumulation for industrialization. In less than 30 years of industrialization, the accumulation
rate has reached as high as $30\% \sim 40\%$ in most years, and before the
reform and opening up, the accumulation amount provided by agriculture maintained at an average of 40% [1]. In this way, under the promotion of the state's catching up strategy, cities and industries have been
given priority to develop while rural areas and agriculture have become
the basis for the primitive accumulation of industrialization. As a result,
China's urban-rural dual economic structure has been formed. What is
compatible with this is the urban-rural dual financial structure endogenous to the strategic needs and the de facto dual social structure of ur-

---

[1] Zou Lixing, Development Finance and Sustainable Development[M]. Hunan University Press, 128.

ban and rural governance.

Such a urban-rural dual structure of economy, finance and society has become a bottleneck for the further development of China, and thus the coordinated development of urban and rural areas is an inevitable choice. There are many underlying reasons for the formation and development of urban-rural dual financial structure, which include not only the initial national strategies and rural financial repression, but also the different levels of development in urban and rural areas and the differences in urban and rural industrial structure. Besides, rural finance is difficult to grow under the rural financial control by local governments.

Driven by the initial national strategy, industrialization and economy in cities develop very fast, which is in sharp contrast with the rural economy where capital and resources have been withdrawn. An urban-rural dual economic structure is formed, and finance subordinate to the national economic strategy also shows duality. The differential treatment between urban and rural residents in finance has manifested the will of the government and has been partly caused by path dependence, but it mainly reflects the economic laws. Tracking the formation of the dual structure of China's economy in history, it can be seen that the financial development in China also shows dualistic feature. Suppression of rural finance in both supply and demand has exacerbated the intensification of urban-rural dual financial structure.

With the implementation of the tax distribution system and the competition in economic development among local governments, local governments' control over rural finance has restricted the self-development of rural finance and rendered rural finance non-market-oriented and vulnerable under intense government intervention. The economic growth in rural areas is too limited to support the financial system as large-scale and high-cost as those in the cities. Rural areas can only develop rural financial systems corresponding to the low-level rural economy. In short, the differences between urban and rural economic development are the root cause of the urban-rural dual financial structure.

4.1.3 Main Demanders of Inclusive Finance in China: Demand-oriented Financial Supply

At present, the problem of inclusive finance in China lies in the neglect of the main demands and the misplacement of financial supply. Therefore, developing the inclusive financial demands in China requires analyses of the actual needs of inclusive finance and demand-focused supply of inclusive finance.

The current potential demanders of inclusive finance in China mainly include:

(1) farmers;

(2) low and middle-income urban residents and the urban poor;

(3) small and medium-sized enterprises;

(4) urban start-ups.

Related financial institutions and service systems should focus on these four groups of people, who have diversified demands for financial services. Their demands include credit demand, savings demand, investment demand and insurance demand, and credit demand is by far the most important financial demand. Different groups show different characteristics in their credit demand, so diversified financial institutions and different financial service methods are needed to meet the credit demand of the demanders of inclusive finance.

At present, the above four groups are the main demanders of inclusive finance in China. Therefore, the construction of inclusive financial system should center around these potential clients, and the financial services provided should be able to meet the financial needs of different groups of clients as much as possible. For example, for the group of farmers, the inclusive financial system should provide them with various forms of small credit to meet their basic financial needs, while for SMEs and micro enterprises, the inclusive financial system must meet their diversified financial needs by providing services such as microcredit and commercial credit so as to achieve the inclusive goal of inclusive finance.

The above content is a qualitative analysis of the main demand groups of inclusive finance. By selecting certain indicators and conducting an quantitative analysis of the potential inclusive financial market, it can be found that the development of inclusive finance in China has great potential.

In China's rural economy, the total number of small and medium-sized township enterprises, one of the main demanders of inclusive finance, has been showing strong growth. Although the growth rate has shown fluctuation, it has remained at a positive level. The total number of township enterprises has been increasing, which means that the financial needs of these township enterprises have been growing. This shows that in recent years, the main demanders of inclusive financial services in China have become stronger in their financial demand. Township enterprises have long been a powerful force in the development of China's rural economy. So increasing financial services for rural enterprises can speed up the development of rural economy and contribute to the healthy and stable development of the Chinese society.

Financial development, especially the development of inclusive finance, has a positive effect on narrowing the gap between urban and rural areas and promoting economic development[①]. The development of inclusive finance is an important regulator for the urban-rural differences and the imbalances in China's eastern, central and western regions, and this regulator functions by giving equal market power to urban and rural areas and the eastern and western regions for them to achieve fair results rather than by strengthening or subsidizing.

The direct impact that the urban-rural dual structure has on the sustainable development of inclusive finance is the dual interest rate structure of inclusive financial institutions. The differences between the supply of inclusive finance in urban areas and rural areas have led to different interest rates that inclusive financial institutions charge in urban and rural areas. This has resulted in different operating income and loan loss provisions in urban and rural inclusive financial institutions, which directly leads to the difficulty in measuring the sustainability of inclusive financial institutions.

4.1.4 Sustainability of Urban Inclusive Finance

4.1.4.1 Characteristics of the Supply of Urban Inclusive Finance

China's urban economy is growing at a fast pace. In particular, the city clusters in the eastern region are large with relatively high—level financial development. The main clients of urban inclusive financial services are urban residents, and the main providers of inclusive financial

---

① Huang Yinghui, Li Hong, Li Zhi. Suggestions on Narrowing the Income Gap between Urban and Rural Residents in Chongqing [J]. Journal of Statistics and Decision, 2008 (2): 143—145.

services are regular financial institutions[①], such as policy financial institutions and formal commercial banks. At present, although China's policy banks have entered into the field of inclusive financial services, their contributions to economic development and the financing of inclusive finance have been very limited and their policy-oriented financial functions have not been brought into full play because of insufficient sources of funds, single function orientation and the narrow business scope.

The main providers of urban inclusive financial services are not policy commercial banks and ordinary commercial banks. They do not occupy the main position in urban inclusive finance and can not provide financial services due to lack of impetus. Besides, Internet financial institutions and other emerging institutions have become providers of urban inclusive financial services and they carry out business mainly in the cities as credit and information systems are more developed there. The present issue of the sustainability of urban inclusive finance is mainly about a series of problems caused by the uncontrolled growth of emerging financial institutions and the lack of supervision.

Seen from the FSS of urban inclusive finance's providers, the providers of urban inclusive finance are facing a large number of new population generated in the urbanization process, which will bring a large amount of operating income to urban financial institutions. Besides, due to sound infrastructure and adequate payment means in cities, the financial repression is relatively weak.

---

① Formal financial institutions refer to the financial institutions that are formally established and governed by the government in accordance with the relevant laws and regulations, which include PBOC, policy banks, commercial banks, cooperative financial organizations and other financial institutions.

4.1.4.2 Characteristics of the Demand for Urban Inclusive Finance

The demand of urban residents in China is mainly reflected in consumer finance and the convenient technical services. For urban residents, especially urban low-income earners, their fixed demand for renting houses, purchasing appliances, house decoration, medical care and education should be met. Besides, considering the faster-paced life in urban areas, inclusive finance should provide urban residents with convenient services such as a payment service to pay living expenses like utilities so as to let them enjoy a convenient lifestyle in cities.

The main demanders of inclusive finance in urban areas are mainly SMEs, micro enterprises and small businesses, which are characterized by small operation scale, small capital flow and nonstandard management. Therefore, when SMEs and micro enterprises need bank loans, they are often faced with difficulties and can not meet the loan requirements of state-owned banks. Even if the loan requirements are met, SMEs and micro enterprises also have to face the high costs. According to the latest CBRC statistics, by the end of September 2017, China had a total of about 70 million SMEs, with an average funding gap of 70.5 trillion yuan each, and most of these SMEs were in cities.

4.1.5 Sustainability of Rural Inclusive Finance

4.1.5.1 Characteristics of Rural Inclusive Finance

In rural China, due to the risks of inclusive finance, the return on investment funds is not high, and many of the funds are used for non-profit-making purposes, making it hard for rural financial institutions to bear the high cost of capital. Compared with market-oriented finance, many inclusive financial demands have become ineffective financial demands without market support, as they can hardly get sufficient financial support from formal financial organizations. Hence, private financing has become an important source and method to meet the demands of inclusive finance.

Informal financial institutions include private lending[1], mutual aid associations, agents, etc.

There are several characteristics of private lending:

(1)private lending usually takes place between acquaintances, such as friends or family members, who gradually form a closely linked network of credit relations, greatly reducing the risk of information asymmetry;

(2)private lending is usually short-term lending, and is more flexible as interest rates are discussed and decided by the lenders and borrowers;

(3)applying for private lending is convenient and is a short process.

Private lending is an informal form of financial organization and is very common in China. Private lending includes loans and guarantees between relatives and friends. Fund demand in private lending is mainly borrowing demand from relatives and friends with low loan interests, showing features of mutual assistance. Other forms of private lending

---

[1] Private lending refers to the civil act between natural persons and enterprises. According to the agreement, the lenders transfer a certain amount of funds to the borrowers, and the borrowers repay the loan and interest as payment comes due.

can be seen in ROSCA[①] fund raising[②], private banks (known as Qianzhuang in China)[③] and other informal financing organizations. ROSCA is a form of private financing that has a long history in China. Private lending forms also include agents, various credit agencies, mutual aid associations and savings banks. Agents and various credit agencies are individuals or institutions that are entrusted with credit business in remote rural areas where there are no branch of formal financial insti-

---

① Rotating savings and credit association (ROSCA) refers to a group of individuals who regularly meet for a defined period so as to save money and borrow together. Members of ROSCA are usually bonded by blood or geographic relations. Each member periodically contributes a certain amount of funds at each meeting, and one member keeps the whole funds once. After each member accesses the funds, ROSCA is dissolved. This type of informal financial organizations is usually small in size. At present, ROSCA has developed into a large-scale, comprehensive profit-making association with high monthly interest. With economic development and diversified financial needs, ROSCA has been rapidly developing. The purpose of joining ROSCA is not only purely for mutual assistance in emergencies, but also to obtain high interest income.

② Fund raising is a way of direct financing. It normally refers to the process of gathering social idle funds based on the principle of free will and mutual benefit. It is sometimes used to refer to the identification and solicitation of investors or other sources of capital for for-profit enterprises. Most fund-raising activities occur in township and village enterprises and private-owned enterprises, and most funds are requested from the employees in the enterprises. The funds is mainly used to solve the problems of insufficient fixed capital and working capital to purchase equipment. Based on the level of interest rates, fund raising can be divided into interest-free fund raising, low-interest fund raising and high-interest fund raising; according to its purposes, fund raising can be divided into non-productive fund raising, productive and operational fund raising; fund raising can also be divided into different forms according to different fund raisers.

③ Private banks are common in Zhejiang and Fujian provinces where commodity economy is more developed. Private banks mainly manage deposits and loans. Compared with decentralized private lending, private banks are more advantageous in scale and credit. From the perspective of organizational form, private banks are normally run by family members, which has made the transactions simple, fast and low-cost. Private banks develop business in the acquaintance network and serve relatively stable clients. At present, although the number and scope of private banks that are active is limited, the financing scale is large.

tutions. Mutual aid association and mutual aid savings union generally do not require official recognition, and they play a role similar to that of the rural foundation.

Table 4.1 Characteristics of Rural Inclusive Finance

Credit Demander	Credit Demand	Credit Provider
Rural poor households	Basic living expenses, small-scale farming	Lending from friends and relatives, private microcredit, small commercial loans
Subsistence rural households	Production PH	Credit, policy-oriented poverty alleviation loans, policy finance
Market-oriented rural households	Market demand	Own funds, commercial credit, private credit
Seed enterprises	Expanding scale	commercial credit, venture capital
Small and micro enterprises	Expanding scale	Free funds, commercial credit
Middle-sized enterprises	Expanding scale and gaining RTS	Investment, commercial credit, policy finance
Leading enterprises	Sustainability	Commercial credit, policy finance
Rural grass-roots government	Infrastructure	Financial budget

Source: Zhu Jian. Research on the Reconstruction of China's rural financial system [M]. Social Sciences Literature Publishing House, 2008.

On the whole, private finance has a direct relationship with regional differences and the development degrees of private economy. In traditional agricultural areas where economy is underdeveloped or moderately developed, the forms of private finance are mainly traditional free lending and private fund raising, whose purpose is mainly to meet people's needs of daily production and living. Whereas in the economically developed areas, the demands for funds are stronger and more popular, and the forms of private finance are more organized, developing towards the forms of ROSCA and private banks which have more obvious features of modern finance. This regional difference in private finance is closely related to the differences in financial demands of economic entities in different regions. Hence, private finance can be defined as a type of "endogenous finance" spontaneously formed to solve the financial demands of economic entities for production and living in certain geographical areas.

4.1.5.2 Credit Cooperatives and Village Banks in Rural Economy

Cooperative financial institutions are a branch of the cooperative economy. They are based on the principle of cooperation, stick to financial principle, and take the special commodity of money as the management object. Cooperative financial institutions have the dual nature of cooperatives and financial organizations, and have realized the financial cooperation among laborers, which is different from the production cooperation based on the production alliance, the supply and marketing cooperation based on production, the livelihood exchange between the supply and demand sides, and the consumptive cooperation based on the purchase of consumer goods, etc. At the same time, cooperative financial institutions are also a branch of financial enterprises. They are funded by individuals or groups and formed mainly to serve their shareholders. The democratic management of cooperative financial institutions is different from the commercial operation of joint-stock banks, or that of policy banks providing policy-oriented financial services, or the commercial management of state-owned commercial banks.

In accordance with the requirements of the modern financial enterprise system, the cooperative financial organizations have gradually perfected the rules of procedure under the instruction of CBRC, CSRC and CIRC and have initially formed a corporate governance system with decision making, implementation and supervision in checks and balances, significantly improving the quality of assets and enhancing the profitability. However, there are still a series of issues to be resolved, such as poorly structured ownership, nominal subject of property rights, and insider control. Besides, the corporate governance structure, operating mechanism and management system needs to be further improved.

In products and services, the cooperative financial organizations provide only limited types of credit and one single mode of guarantee. The adjustment of credit orientation is not made in time, and the deployment of intermediary business is slow. In addition, the construction of information technology has been lagging behind, and the settlement channels are impeded. Payment and settlement methods are still dominated by traditional settlement like cash settlement, and the coverage of credit cards, bills and other advanced tools is still very low. The cooperative financial organizations generally do not conduct international settlement business and trade financing business, and thus are unable to meet the demand for financial services of export-oriented enterprises.

In interest rate pricing, the cooperative financial organizations haven't established an effective, flexible and scientific loan pricing mechanism. Although in some areas they have implemented different interest rate management measures, the problems of lacking market awareness and much subjectivity in loan pricing are still prominent.

In terms of asset quality, the cooperative financial organizations are facing problems like poor asset quality, heavy financial burden, etc.

4.1.5.3 Semi-formal Inclusive Financial Institutions in Rural Economy

In the situation of rural economic development, private financing in rural economy is the main part of private financial activities, which are geographically concentrated and continuous in time dimension. Except for certain private bank financing and internal financing in private enterprises, most private financial activities are decentralized with a low degree of organization and marketization.

With the advancement in financial reform, the scale of direct financing has been gradually expanded, interest rate control has been relaxed, and the role of the market in the allocation of financial resources has been strengthened. In this context, the external environment for the survival and development of private financing has been improved, and the degree of acceptance and recognition of private financing in the entire economic society has also been raised.

4.1.6 Rural Areas: Priority Areas in Dealing with the Issue of the Sustainability of Inclusive finance in China

In dealing with the current issue of the sustainability of inclusive finance in China, the main problem is that a considerable number of people in rural areas, poor areas and farmer groups can not get access to financial services. The Central Document No. 1 issued out in consecutive 7 years from 2004 to 2010 introduced relevant policies for the development of new rural financial institutions in China that aimed to establish an inclusive financial system in China, with the goal of meeting the multi—level financial needs in rural areas.

As an effective method of poverty alleviation, rural microfinance is an important practice of current rural financial reform, which is in line with the current development direction of financial support for agriculture in China. At present, the pilot established new rural microfinance institutions in China, which can be mainly divided into three operational modes: village banks, microcredit companies and rural capital cooperatives.

Village banks are launched by big banks, funded by investors, and coordinated by the government. Village banks are applicable to rural economy which suffers from large loss of funds, prominent contradiction among fund supply and demand, insufficient competition and inadequate services. Village banks enjoy the advantages of flexible management mechanism and quick loans, but they also have shortcomings. As village banks were established more later, and have dispersed clients and fewer branches, it is very difficult for village banks to organize deposits in the rural market; the scope of business and the types of financial products of village banks are limited, and services can only be provided to one county or one town; the initial document clearly stated that the required capital for opening a village bank is 1 million to 3 million yuan, making it difficult for village banks to enjoy agricultural re-loans. By December 2015, there were 1,519 rural banks that were newly established in China[1].

---

[1] Peng Xiangsheng. Research on the Development of Inclusive Finance in Rural China [M]. Fuzhou Normal university Press, 2016.

Microcredit companies are non-bank financial institutions established by domestic commercial banks or rural cooperative banks to operate credit-only microcredit business. Microcredit companies are an innovation in promoting inclusive finance targeted at China's national conditions. They are suitable for rural areas with huge potential for economic development and large credit balances. Microcredit companies are flexible enough to meet the "small and decentralized" credit service requirements of farmers and micro enterprises, but the business of microcredit companies is vulnerable as it faces constraints from funding banks' assets, small wholesale funds and supporting service pilot finance companies.

Table 4.2 Information of Agriculture-related
Financial Institutions in 2014

Institution	2014		
	Number of institutions	Number of branches	Number of employees
Rural credit cooperatives	1596	42201	423992
Rural commercial banks	665	32776	373635
Rural cooperative bank	89	3269	32614
Village bank	1153	3088	58935
Loan company	14	14	148
Rural capital cooperative	49	49	521
Total	3566	81397	889845

Source: www.cbrc.gov.cn

Rural capital cooperative organizations are microfinance institutions voluntarily formed by farmers, individual businesses, small and micro-sized enterprises and professional cooperatives under the principle of co-operation and only provide services to their members. Rural capital co-operative organizations are suitable for industries or regions with insufficient formal financial services or considerable professional cooperation. Rural capital cooperative organizations have the advantages of localization, low operating costs, simple loan procedures and low interest rates. However, rural capital cooperative organizations' scale of loans is small, making them unable to meet the needs for large-scale, long-term funds. In addition, rural capital cooperative organizations also lack of management capacity.

Although the national policies strongly support the development of rural financial institutions, there are still many difficulties in the development of microfinance institutions in rural areas, affecting the sustainability of microfinance. The main constraints are as follows: insufficient follow-up funds, mismatched sources and terms of funds; underdeveloped client credit system; unclear legal status.

4.1.7 Inclusive Finance in Urban and Rural Areas

In view of the overall development of inclusive finance in recent years, although all kinds of inclusive financial supply modes have emerged in urban and rural areas, there are obvious structural features and differences in the overall supply structure. Emerging Internet finance dominates the urban inclusive financial market, whereas the rural inclusive finance mainly focuses on microcredit and rural banks and most rural areas depend on some informal inclusive financial models besides microcredit and rural banks. Therefore, in order to break these differences in financial structure, it is necessary to enhance the supervision on urban inclusive finance companies, to lead, funds to flow to rural areas, and to accelerate the process of the formalization of inclusive financial institutions in rural areas.

Table 4.3 Inclusive Finance Models in Urban and Rural Areas

	Urban inclusive finance	Rural inclusive finance
Main provider	Formal banks; Inclusive financial institutions	Inclusive financial institutions; Semi-formal institutions; Informal inclusive financial institutions; Village banks; Regional banks
Main demand	Financial demand of small and micro-sized enterprises; Consumer finance; Convenient payment	Farmers' productive expenditure and fixed expenditure; Financial demand of small and micro-sized enterprises
Major problem	Insufficient funds of small and micro-sized enterprise; Systemic risk	Significant outflow of funds; High costs; High vulnerability; Lack of vitality

Source: www.cbrc.gov.cn

4.2 Sustainability of Inclusive Finance in China's Process of Urbanization

China's urban-rural dual financial structure has not been transformed with China's reform and opening up and economic growth. Instead, the actual situation shows that there is a tendency of the intensification of the urban-rural dual financial structure, which has been prominent especially after the mid-to-late 1990s.

4.2.1 Urban-rural Dual Structure is Anti-urbanization

Judging from the relevant indicators of urban and rural economic development, there is a clear gap between urban and rural areas, which is mainly reflected in:

(1)the gap between economic growth rate of rural and urban economy;

(2)the widened absolute income gap and relative income gap between urban and rural residents;

(3)the widened absolute consumption gap and relative consumption gap between urban and rural residents;

(4)"the Matthew effect" in urban and rural economic growth and economic efficiency;

(5)the widening gap between urban and rural areas;

(6)larger Gini coefficient.

In the financial aspect, China's finance has two relatively independent and financial sectors, namely, rural finance that represents the traditional sectors and urban finance that represents the modern sectors. The current financial relationship between urban and rural areas in China can be basically summed up as the dual financial structure accompanying the urban-rural dual economic structure.

The process of urbanization is accompanied by the developing process of urban industrialization and requires a large amount of labor force to participate as well as the cooperation of high-level secondary and tertiary industries. However, the urban-rural dual structure has been impeding this process. Therefore, the process of urbanization requires the elimination of the urban-rural dual structure and the utilization of the rural elements and resources in the process of urbanization.

4.2.2 Urbanization: Fundamental Way out for Rural Inclusive Finance

The rural financial system consists of commercial finance, cooperative finance and policy finance, but the number and power of financial institutions in rural areas are far less than those in the cities. In the aspect of financial markets, the rural areas are characterized by single credit market, whereas the urban financial market includes the direct financial markets and indirect financial markets.

Urban-rural dual financial structure has a profound impact on urban and rural economic development, urban and rural overall strategies and urban and rural industrial structure adjustment. There is a huge gap between the financial development in urban and rural areas, which will inevitably impact urban and rural economic development, and thus strengthen the urban-rural dual economic structure. In this case, the income gap between urban and rural residents will be difficult to be narrowed, the gap between regional economic development will be constantly expanding, and the predicament of the separated development of industrialization and urbanization is hard to change.

Under urban-rural dual financial structure, rural financial development has been greatly inhibited, as the overall rural financial assets is limited, the types of financial services are scarce, the financing channels are narrow, and urban financial intermediaries and financial market can not or will not provide financial services to rural financial entities, which has intensified the imbalance between supply and demand in rural finance.

From the perspective of financial function, the rural areas lack not so much financial institutions as financial function. This lack makes the role of finance in promoting the allocation of resources in rural areas less obvious, thus aggravating the income gap between urban and rural areas. With underdeveloped rural finance and small scale of credit funds, the rural industrial structure can hardly be strategically adjusted, and the rural economic structure can hardly be transformed qualitatively. Furthermore, the industrial structure and economic structure in urban and rural areas can hardly be changed within a short period of time.

Urbanization can bring two results to rural finance: first, urbanization will raised the overall demand effectively and is therefore a great boost to rural and agricultural development; second, urbanization will effectively strengthen the connection between urban and rural areas and enhance the sustainability of rural demands.

According to Xu Dixin's research, every 1% increase in China's urbanization rate can boost GDP by at least 1.5%, which can not be a-chieved by rural economic development. The National Bureau of Statistics shows that the urbanization rate of China's permanent population in 2015 was 56.1%, and the urbanization rate of China's permanent population in western regions was 48.7% (The 13th Five-Year Plan for Western Development).

Table 4.4 China's Urbanization Rate in 2014

Region	East	Center	West
Urbanization rate	62.2%	48.5%	44.8%

Source: www.cbrc.gov.cn

According to the analysis by Yao Yang, dean and professor of National Development Research Institute of Peking University, the urbanization rate of the permanent population in the eastern region is currently close to 70%, while that in the central and western regions is only about 50%, a difference of 20%, which means a 15-to-20 years' gap[①].

Therefore, major development in rural areas at present is both unrealistic and unreasonable. China should maintain the inclusive finance in rural areas based on the present population and household registration system. The ultimate goal of China's inclusive finance is large-scale urbanization. The process of urbanization have generated many problems, but the positive impact that urbanization has brought about should not be denied. Hence, when considering the issue of inclusive finance in rural areas, China must take into account the future platform for rural inclusive finance to dock with urban inclusive finance so as to achieve the transformation from serving the farmers to serving the citizens. If China neglects this, large amounts of investment will become precipitated capital once China's urbanization is completed and huge amounts of demands for rural inclusive finance change. The establishment and development of village banks have embodied such a forward-looking approach. Under the promotion of the CBRC, a large number of

---

① Zhao Yanqing. City has played a leading role in promoting economic development [M]. China Reform News, 2002.

rural credit cooperatives have been reorganized into village banks and modernized corporate governance has been adopted to establish inclusive financial institutions so that when farmers become new citizens and agricultural processing industry expand, they can still receive corresponding inclusive financial services. This is a path of sustainable development that will help achieve common progress in China.

4.3 Advantages in China's Inclusive Finance: Late-mover Advantages with the Development of Information Technology

"The development of information technology is changing people's lives and especially finance profoundly."[1] Finance is a special industry based on information and confidence. The development of information technology has reduced the transaction costs, accelerated the commodity exchange and significantly promoted the capability of allocating financial resources across time and space.

(1) The fundamental factors of credit intermediaries have changed. Credit risk has undergone major changes in the credit process. Before, banks' assessment of a person's credit when offering loans was mainly based on his/her past repayment performance and financial information; now, it is also based on the data of his/her consumption, travels, taxes, traffic violations and even WeChat Moments, getting a full-scale understanding of this person from various information dimensions. As far as inclusive finance is concerned, the problem of asymmetric information has been greatly eased, and thus the basic banking service model based on collateral is changed.

---

[1] 2017—12—17 10:01:19 China Securities Online

(2) Pricing of financial products has changed from fuzzy interest rate pricing to precise pricing. With full understanding of the information, credit is regarded no longer as a static point, but as a multidimensional space, a dynamic curve and an accurate point-to-point mapping. The new pricing model has changed the previous model of unified pricing and has put higher requirements on pricing capabilities of commercial institutions. At the same time, it is also a bargaining process for inclusive finance demanders, that is, on the supply and demand curve, the providers can maximize the consumer surplus after expanding the coverage.

(3) The use of information technology in the post-loan stage can clearly indicate the flow of loans. This Visualized process can show which note the loans flow to and what type of transactions is being conducted, and thus effectively reduce moral hazard and achieve efficient functioning of inclusive financial system, thereby enhancing the anti-risk capability and profitability of inclusive finance.

"With pre-loan transparency, full-dimensional credit system, accurate pricing and fully transparent post-loan process, the credit risk will be greatly reduced."[1] For inclusive finance marked by microcredit, the construction of credit system is more effective than traditional credit instruments such as mortgage guarantees. Microfinance and consumer finance will become a "Blue Ocean" as long as the issue of credit risk is solved and transaction costs are reduced. Moreover, financial innovation will also bring about tremendous changes in commercial banks, which will gradually evolve into data-based institutions, and bring slow but huge changes in the entire financial ecology.

---

[1] Fan Wenzhong. Director of International Department, China Banking Regulatory Commission.

Therefore, the development of inclusive finance in China is realized with the integration of traditional inclusive finance and internet technology and is equipped with obvious late-mover advantages[1]. But it is to a certain extent troubled with issues caused by later-mover disadvantages[2]. Later-mover advantages mean that China can learn from the existing experience of developed western countries and other developing countries to promote the development of its own inclusive finance, whereas late-mover disadvantages mean that while focusing on the rapid development of inclusive finance, China may fail to pay enough attention to the regulations and system constructions of inclusive finance. This will result in a lack of stamina in inclusive finance and hindering its sustainable development, of which a recent series of risk events of inclusive finance in China have provided alarming examples.

4.4 Existing Problems in China's Inclusive Financial System

4.4.1 Outstanding Problems of Urban Inclusive Finance

Table 4.5 Closed Internet Financial Platforms and Problem Platforms

Time	Number of closed platforms and problem platforms	Number of investors involved (10,000)	X% of the total investors	Amount of loan balance involved (100 million yuan)	X% of the total loan balance
2013	93	1.6	6.4%	16.1	6.0%
2014	394	6.3	5.4%	68.2	6.6%

---

① Yang Xiaokai. New Classical Economics[M]. Business Press, 2002.

② Industry Development Report on China's Microcredit Companies, 2005—2016.

Continued

Time	Number of closed platforms and problem platforms	Number of investors involved (10,000)	X% of the total investors	Amount of loan balance involved (100 million yuan)	X% of the total loan balance
2015	1688	27.7	4.7%	171.1	4.2%
2016	3429	45.2	4.5%	258.1	3.2%
2017	4008	55.7	3.7%	322.4	2.7%

Source: WDZJ Research Center

Internet financial platforms represented by p2p platforms are the main providers of urban inclusive finance. In recent years, with the explosive growth of financial institutions, the number of closed Internet financial platforms and problem platforms in China has been increasing. By November 2017, there were 4,008 problem platforms with 557,000 people involved and a loan amount of 32.24 billion yuan, which had an impact on the stability of China's entire financial system. Therefore, the biggest problem for inclusive finance in China's urban areas is regulating internet inclusive financial companies to reduce their negative impact on the financial system.

4.4.2 Insufficient Rural Funds

Insufficient follow-up funds are one of the three major factors impeding the development of agriculture[①]. There is a great demand for funds in rural areas, but different types of microfinance institutions in

---

① Shen Yan. Development and Transformation of China's Formal Finance at the Rural Level[M]. Peking University Press, 190.

rural areas are all troubled with the problem of insufficient follow-up funds. As village banks were established more later with fewer branches and inadequate supporting measures for operation and development, most village banks have so far failed to obtain enough funds to sustain their development.

Seen from the credit and capital flow in China, capital in China mainly flows from the countryside to the cities, and the demand for funds in rural areas of China has not been met for a long time. In addition, due to the flow of population to the cities, the funds in rural areas are in a state of net expenditure. Therefore, in order to maintain the balance of rural funds, China must control rural funds in terms of total amount and dynamic changes. In recent years, PBOC has always been giving preferential policies on agriculture-related funds when regulating monetary policies, which has given positive promotion for the sustainable development of inclusive finance at the government level.

4.4.3 Government Laws, Policies and Regulation: China's Practical Problems

Since the beginning of the 21st century, three major changes in the Chinese government's goals have profoundly affected the development of inclusive finance: cleaning up and reorganizing the banking system, promoting social harmony and preventing the spread of the global financial crisis[1].

Under China's financial system, China's government laws, policies and regulations have a decisive external influence on the develop-

---

[1] Inclusive Financial Situation in the People's Republic of China, 2012 CGAP Work Report.

ment of inclusive finance. However, while the government is promoting the rapid development of inclusive finance, the late-mover disadvantages also manifest, such as the poor management under market impact, and systemic risks and absconding when certain inclusive financial institutions are maliciously exploited by their shareholders.

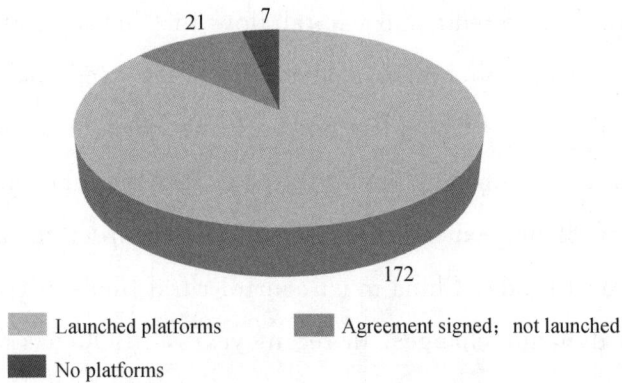

Figure 4.1 Statistics of the Storage and Management Platforms of the Top 200 Banks in China

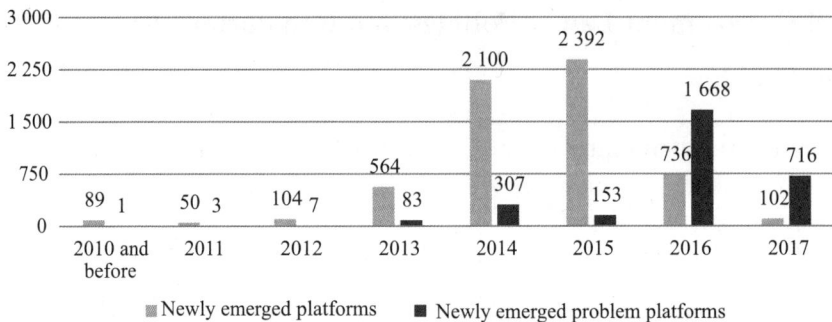

Source: 2017 Report on the Development of China's Inclusive Finance

Figure 4.2 Development Situation of New Internet Finance Platforms in China from 2010 to 2017

With the great growth of Internet finance, China has enjoyed a period of rapid development of inclusive finance. In this process, various funds have joined the inclusive financial market one by one and established a large number of internet inclusive financial platforms through the use of Internet technology. However, the number of problem platforms are increasing, which is caused by the fact that the regulatory system in China is disjointed from the actual situation.

The main problems are:

(1) The rich return on capital of the internet inclusive financial platforms has brought about rapid market growth. Due to the significantly higher interest rates and low entry requirements for setting up a company, both domestic and foreign hot money and private funds have entered the inclusive financial market with obvious profit motives, which will affect the entire ecosystem;

(2) Over-findebtedness will lead to systemic risks. Over-indebtedness is the biggest problem facing the global microfinance industry[1]. Fierce competition in the market has prompted institutions to loosen their lending conditions, resulting in serious consequences, such as overreaction of policymakers, suspicions about the purpose and motivation of inclusive finance, etc., which not only hinders the development of microfinance institutions but and creates a series of social problems[2].

---

[1] Global Financial Innovation Research Center, Global Microcredit Finance Banana Skins, 2016.

[2] The microcredit crisis in Pakistan, Bosnia, Herzegovina and other countries in 2010 was caused by its fast-growing operational model. See 2016 Report on the Development of China's Microfinance Companies, 43.

4.5 Summary

Dynamic inclusive financial sustainability is essentially a matter of matching the risks and benefits in the inclusive financial system. The systemic risk of inclusive finance stems from the liberalization of interest rates after financial deepening and under the impact of emerging technologies, which makes the traditional inclusive financial institutions unable to guarantee financial sustainability. Besides, the sharp increase or decrease of the demand for inclusive financial services will also affect the sustainability of inclusive finance. Still, the rising poverty standards have brought sustained impetus to the demand for inclusive financial services.

Moreover, the inclusive financial system is only a small part of the big financial system. The demand and supply of inclusive financial services are subject to the constraints of the big financial system, and inclusive financial services are bound to be constrained by the overall financial demand and supply. In addition, with gradually mature individual right system, inclusive finance will inevitably face more regulatory and institutional constraints. Hence, to ensure the sustainability of inclusive finance in China requires the foresight at multiple levels.

China's inclusive financial sustainable development possess both the common features of inclusive financial development and its own unique characteristics, that is, due to the late starting and fast development of inclusive finance in China as well as the existing infrastructure and demographic dividend, China's inclusive financial infrastructure has adopted the latest technological achievements and thus possesses late-mover advantages in some fields and has provided a platform for other countries in the world to study.

Still, it should not be neglected that as urban-rural dual structure still exists in China and China is still in the process of rapid urbanization, the inclusive financial services coming along with new technologies are a double-edged sword. Inclusive financial services have promoted the rapid development and transformation of China's economy and improved common welfare. But at the same time, they have also magnified the possible risks brought by inclusive finance and the impact of inclusive financial system on financial system risk. Hence, to capitalize on the opportunity of inclusive finance in China, China should administer inclusive finance in the legal system and learn from the experience and lessons of other countries, and make contributions to the world's inclusive finance based on China's reality.

To maintain the sustainable development of China's inclusive finance under a dynamic and changing environment, (attention should be paid to the dynamic factors that are affecting China's inclusive finance and the protection of inclusive finance should be strengthened.) The inclusive financial providers should enhance their ability to identify risks, reduce losses and reduce transaction costs, so as to obtain high FSS value. For the demand side of inclusive finance, their ability to obtain funds should be enhanced. The poor should be included into the network of labor division and cooperation through the spillover effect of inclusive finance so as to become consistent demanders of inclusive finance. For the external impact of science and technology on inclusive finance, the government must first empower science and technology to provide support to inclusive finance and to help the construction of the inclusive financial system. The government should also clarify the status of new financial technology companies and guard them against possible risks. The government has given a legal definition that a microcredit company is a non-financial institution and can only use free capital or financing to issue loans or provide information intermediary services. Thus, as credit companies, P2P platforms can only provide financial services within this range and shall not break into the forbidden zones and cause dynamic risks.

Chapter 5   Model Construction and Empirical Analysis

5.1 Definition of the Sustainability of Inclusive Financial Institutions

At present, most researchers agree that the sustainable development of inclusive financial institutions should mainly be measured in terms of financial sustainability. That is, a financially sustainable institution's operating income should be able to make up for the costs to achieve independent development.

Seen from the financial sustainability, the costs of inclusive financial institutions can be broadly classified into three categories. The first is operational cost, which mainly relates to the expenses and costs in the core businesses of inclusive financial institutions. The second is risk cost, which is directly related to the provision for bad loans. The third is the financing cost, which mainly involves the costs of various market-oriented capital sources. Vento (2006) classified the sustainability of inclusive financial institutions into four different types based on the matching between income and costs.

(1)Subsidies dependency

Inclusive financial institutions with subsidies dependency can not cover their operating costs with the operating income. These institutions are unable to make use of compensated funds and their continued operation depends substantially on various subsidies.

(2) Operational self-sufficiency

Operational self-sufficiency is where inclusive a financial institution's operating income is sufficient to cover the operating costs with slight surplus. In such case, institutions have lower reliance on subsidies and can make use of the compensated funds. However, because their income is not sufficient to cover the provision cost, the sustainability of these institutions is relatively fragile and vulnerable to economic fluctuations.

(3) Fully operational self-sufficiency

With fully operational self-sufficiency, inclusive financial institutions can cover with income the operating cost as well as the provision cost. Under such circumstances, the sustainability of the microfinance institutions is strong, and institutions can not only to a large extent get rid of the dependence on subsidies, but also withstand certain economic fluctuations. However, as the profitability of such institutions is not strong enough to utilize market-oriented funds, the development scale of such institutions will be subject to certain restrictions.

(4) Fully financial self-sufficiency

Financial self-sufficiency refers to the situation where income is sufficient to cover the full costs, including the costs of using marketized capital. In this situation, institutions can achieve sustainable development relying on market mechanism. While these institutions are growing in size and in the number of clients, they are also bringing benefits and profits to their creditors and shareholders.

It should be noticed that the above division of the level of sustainable development is based solely on the examination at the financial level and does not imply that certain institutions are superior, because of the differences in countries and clients, the requirements for the sustainable development of inclusive financial institutions may vary greatly.

According to the definition of CGAP (World Bank Consultative Group to Assist the Poor), the financial analysis ratio of inclusive financial institutions consists of 15 indicators in three groups: loan quality ratio, financial yield ratio and profitability ratio[①].

Table 5.1 CGAP Financial Ratio Analysis

	Indicator	Formula
Loan quality ratio	Overdue loan ratio	Total overdue loans/overdue loan balances
	Loan loss ratio	Bad debt loss/average loan balances
	Risky loan ratio	Overdue loan balances/loan balances
Financial productivity ratio	Operating efficiency	
	Management efficiency	
	Personnel cost ratio	
	Average loan accounts of employees	
	Average loan accounts of loan officers	
	Average loans of the institution	
	Average loan balances of loan officers	

---

① Indicators defined by CGAP are more authoritative and comprehensive compared with indicators defined by other organizations.

Continued

	Indicator	Formula
	Adjusted net ROA	
	Adjusted ROA	
Profitability ratio	Loan yield ratio	
	OSS	
	FSS	

Source: www.cbrc.gov.cn

The sustainable development ratio focuses mainly on OSS (operational self-sufficiency index) and FSS (financial self-sufficiency index) in the table above.

In terms of the trends of inclusive finance, the fourth type, full financial self-sufficiency, has become a widely accepted indicator of the sustainability of inclusive financial institutions, which can be indicated by OSS and FSS[1].

$$oss = ly \div (finco + opco + llp)$$

LY = NL * AvLz. It represents the reported annual profit of MFIs. FINCO refers to financial costs, OPCO refers to operating costs, LLP refers to loan loss provision. In general, if OSS>1, it means that the institution's revenue is sufficient to cover all of its expenses and that the institution has "operational self-sufficiency".

$$fss = ly \div (finco + opco + llp + cc)$$

CC represents capital costs, CC={inflation rate * (average total assets-average fixed assets)} + {average total liabilities * market debt rates-actual financial cost}. It is clear that only when FSS>1, institu-

---

[1] Zhang Zhengping. Research on the Sustainable Development of MFIs in China, 169.

tions can have financial sustainability, or "financial self—sufficiency".

It can be seen that FSS can more comprehensively reflect the financial sustainability of the institution than OSS when related comprehensive financial costs have been added, and thus FSS is suggested to be used in future financial evaluation and measurement of inclusive financial institutions.

5.2 Model Construction

Hulme and Mosley pointed out in 1996 that output and profit model could be used to measure the determinants of MFI's sustainability if the MFI was regarded as a traditional institution where input determined the output. Based on Luka Jovita Okumu's sustainable development model (2007), the constructed model of this paper is as follows:

$$ln\ OSS_{it} = C + \beta_1 lnDE\ R_{it} + \beta_2 ln\ GOLP_{it} + \beta_3 ln\ GINDEX_{it} +$$
$$\beta_4 ln\ AvLz_{it} + \beta_5 ln\ RELRD_{it} + \beta_6 ln\ CLD_{it} + \beta_7 ln\ WL_{it} + \beta_8 ln\ AGE_{it} +$$
$$\beta_9 ln\ AREA_{it} + \mu_{it}$$

$$ln\ FSS_{it} = C + \beta_1 lnDE\ R_{it} + \beta_2 ln\ GOLP_{it} + \beta_3 ln\ GINDEX_{it} +$$
$$\beta_4 ln\ AvLz_{it} + \beta_5 ln\ RELRD_{it} + \beta_6 ln\ CLD_{it} + \beta_7 ln\ WL_{it} + \beta_8 ln\ AGE_{it} +$$
$$\beta_9 ln\ AREA_{it} + \mu_{it}$$

Table 5.2 Formula and Expected Correlation of Variables in the Model

Variable	Formula	Expected Correlation
OSS	ly/(finco + opco + llp)	
DER	debt/equity	+ positive correlation
GOLP	gross loan portfolio/total assets	− negative correlation
GINDEX	effectiveness of governance	+ positive correlation

Continued

Variable	Formula	Expected Correlation
AvLz (average loan size)	loan per capita/national per capita income	+ positive correlation
RELRD (real effective lending interest rate)	lending yield rate-inflation rate	+ positive correlation
CLD (unit cost of loans disbursed)	total cost/total loans	− negative correlation
WL	average salaries/wages and benefits in relation to the national per capita income	+ positive correlation
AGE	research time-established time	+ positive correlation
AREA	eastern region=1, central and western regions=0	+ positive correlation

Source: Zhang Zhengping, Research on the Sustainable Development of MFIs in China

(1) Within the regular range, higher DER indicates strong sustainability of the institution; higher GOLP shows weaker capacity to cover costs with assets.

(2) As GINDEX can not be introduced, GINDEX is set as 1 in this model.

(3) AvLz reflects the efficiency of loans.

(4) RELER directly indicates the income level of the MFI.

(5) Higher GLD indicates weaker sustainability.

(6) WL reflects the stability of the MFI. Therefore, some companies deliberately give employees high wages and welfare in order to convey the illusion that their development is stable and sustainable.

(7)AGE proves the continuity of the institutions in the past. Higher AGE indicates that the MFI's model has been tested in the past and its sustainability is more reliable than the emerging companies.

(8)As for AREA, in relatively underdeveloped western areas, the company may be subject to regional factors.

5.3 Empirical Analysis

Quite a number of MFIs in China were established quite late, and their financial records were not comprehensive. Based on the original data of PBOC in 2010 and the statistics disclosed in 2011 Report on the Competitiveness of China's MFIs, Zhang Zhenping (2013)[1] chose 42 representative companies for analysis, the results of which are listed in the tables bellow.

Table 5.3 Descriptive Analysis of 42 MFIs

Indicator	Average	Median	Maximum	Minimum	Standard deviation
OSS	386.76	313.28	1310.04	106.6928	228.82
DER	0.23	0.1528	0.82	−0.0029	0.2360
GOLP	0.00010438	0.0000949	0.0003795	7.02E−05	0.000052
GINDEX	5.7809	5.35	9.5	2.3	2.002954
AvLz	276.05	177.75	1224.94	3.7933	292.4396
RELRD	0.1648	0.1682	0.2198	0.012	0.0318
CLD	0.0392	0.0345	0.1204	0.002569	0.025921

---

[1] Zhang Zhengping. Research on the Sustainable Development of MFIs in China, 193.

Continued

Indicator	Average	Median	Maximum	Minimum	Standard deviation
WL	0.65229556	0.6136	2.322	0.046	0.393
AGE	2.1428	2	3	1	0.60
AREA	0.404720	0	1	0	0.496796

Source: Zhang Zhengping, Research on the Sustainable Development of MFIs in China.

Table 5.4 Analysis of Financial Performance of
42 Sample Companies unit: %

Indicator	OSS	ROA	Net ROA	DER	OPCO ratio
Average	386.76	7.58	9.47	22.84	3.92
Median	313.28	7.40	9.21	15.28	2.71
Maximum	1310.04	16.05	23.67	82.72	12.46
Minimum	106.6928	0.53	0.56	−0.29	0.27

Source: Zhang Zhengping, Research on the Sustainable Development of MFIs in China.

Table 5.5 Results of OSS Regression Estimation

C	lnDER	lnGOLP	lnGINDEX	lnAvLz	lnRELRD	lnCLD	lnWL	lnAGE	lnAREA
−0.645	0.024	−0.504	−0.131	0.07	0.521	−0.70	0.085	0.33	−0.026

Source: Zhang Zhengping, Research on the Sustainable Development of MFIs in China.

Through Zhang Zhenping's analysis, it can be seen that the average financial self-sufficiency of the 42 sample companies in China was over 100%, indicating that they could completely cover their financial costs with revenue. From the cost level, the operating expense ratio was low and the control over costs was relatively strong, helping institutions to improve the profits.

This paper selected 25 Internet platforms as samples for empirical analysis. After data selection, we put info into the model from overall data of Internet P2P platforms in 2017 (see original data in Appendix 1) and measured their FSS based on the related statistics and the regression analysis.

Table 5.6 Descriptive Analysis of the FSS of 25 Internet Platforms

Indicator	FSS	ROA	Net ROA	DER	OPCO ratio
Average	851.36	8.5	10.37	27.44	6.52
Median	151.36	7.9	8.95	14.27	5.11
Maximum	10837.7	12.02	21.63	62.45	15.36
Minimum	1.172	0.25	0.676	−0.7	0.77

Table 5.7 Results of FSS Regression Estimation

C	lnDER	lnGOLP	lnGINDEX	lnAvLz	lnRELRD	lnCLD	lnWL	lnAGE	lnAREA
−0.572	0.04	−0.307	−0.28	0.29	0.487	−0.568	0.105	0.59	−0.192

$$\ln FSS = -0.572 + 0.04\ln DER - 0.307\ln GOLP - 0.28\ln GIND + 0.29\ln AvLz + 0.487\ln RELRD - 0.568\ln CLD + 0.105\ln WL + 0.59\ln AGE - 0.192\ln AREA = 1.2514$$

This value indicates the overall sustainability of P2P platforms in China and proves that the financial sustainability of China's Internet financial platforms is within a health and positive range.

5.4 Summary

(1)CLD, RELRD, AGE, AvLz and GOLP play an important role in OSS. Maintaining sustainability requires improving operational efficiency, reducing loan costs, improving loan yields and achieving scale effect.

(2)AREA is negatively related to OSS. This may be because in the central and western regions, the market competition is not fierce and inclusive finance can thus fill the market gap.

(3) The overall operating efficiency is relatively low. Inclusive financial companies in China must improve the operating efficiency to achieve sustainability.

(4) The sample companies are already relatively well-performing inclusive financial institutions and considering the survivorship bias, the overall picture of grassroots inclusive financial institutions lacking in data may not necessarily be reflected in this analysis.

Chapter 6 Comparative Study on the Inclusive Finance in Indonesia and the Philippines

F or many developing countries, financial inclusion has become the policy objective in economic growth and poverty reduction. Access to financial services is important for every household and business. Inclusive finance therefore carries the objective of improving the well-being of the poor and the growth of micro, small and medium enterprises.

As a developing country in Southeast Asia, the Indonesia has enjoyed the government's support for inclusive finance and financial technology growth. Besides that, while mobile money continues to be in a nascent stage, digital financial service providers view the Indonesia market as having high potential, particularly given the large number of bankable people, geographic conditions, mobile phone ownership levels, government-to-person money flows and growing demand for digital payments. On the other hand, the Philippines is considered as a thought leader in inclusive finance in light of the many initiatives and gains in microfinance and more recently in mobile financial services. Hence, Indonesia and the Philippines are worthy of research and concern on the issue of the sustainability of financial inclusion and may provide reference value for establishing sustainable inclusive finance in China.

Robust, objective and reliable data can provide meaningful insights on the state of financial inclusion that can be used to identify gaps, establish priorities and craft evidence-based policies. The National Strategy for Financial Inclusion issued by the government of Philippines indicates four components of financial inclusion: (1) access; (2) quality; (3) usage; (4) welfare[①]. At present, most of the available financial inclusion datas in Indonesia and the Philippines are on the access and usage dimension while information on quality and welfare is lacking and may not be in sufficient depth to measure financial inclusion. Thus, the level of inclusive finance in Indonesia and the Philippines are measured mainly in regard to the access and usage of the inclusive finance.

6.1 Development of Inclusive Finance in Indonesia

6.1.1 General Situation of Inclusive Finance in Indonesia

Indonesia is the largest economy in Southeast Asia and a member of the G20. As the fourth most populous nation in the world and the largest emerging market, Indonesia has been enjoying a huge demographic dividend. In 2016, Indonesia had a total population of more than 260 million, of which about 35% were under the age of 35, allowing mobile internet to enjoy a higher acceptance in Indonesia[②]. Agriculture, oil and gas industries are the pillar of Indonesia's national economy. However, Indonesia also faces certain social problems: more than half of the population (more than 250 million people) continues to live on less than

---

① Gillbero M. Llanto and Maureen Ane D. Rosellon. "What Determines Financial Inclusion in the Philippines? Evidence from a National Baseline Survey"[J]. Discussion Paper Series, 2017(38).

② https://data.worldbank.org.cn/country/indonesia? view=chart.

$ 2.50 a day[1], the gap between the rich and the poor is huge, and the less developed areas have rather poor conditions.

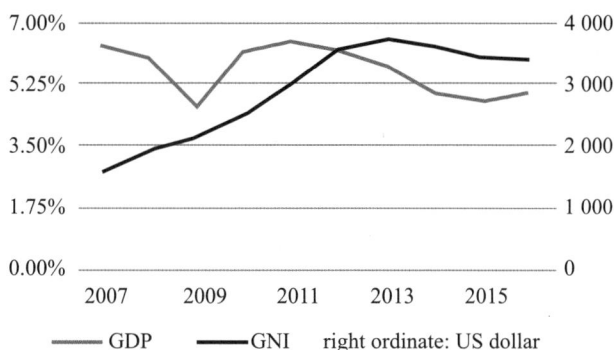

Figure 6.1 GDP and GNI of Indonesia

According to the 2017 Annual Report of Financial Inclusion in Indonesia released by Financial Inclusion Insights, banks remain the driver of Indonesian inclusive finance, and 93% of Indonesian adults who are financially included hold a full-service bank account. The majority of financially included adults have digital access to their account, which is driven by bank account registration. However, mobile money use is still very low among Indonesians. Less than 1% of Indonesia adults have used mobile money. But the awareness of mobile money services rose substantially from 8% in 2015 to 15% of the adult population in 2016. Financial services remain concentrated among the urban, above poverty line and male population and large divides in active account usage persist across poverty status, geography and gender.

As for the access of financial inclusion, 34% of Indonesians in 2016 had access to some form of full-service financial account, and 26% had a registered account.[2] Most Indonesians remain unaware of mobile money

---

[1]　Data from the World Bank

[2]　2017 Annual Report: Financial Inclusion in Indonesia.

and few of them have ever accessed any mobile money service. Banks are viewed more positively than mobile money in terms of convenience, reliability and user control by those that are aware of both services.

Usage of inclusive finance refers to the utilization of different inclusive financial products and services. In Indonesia, financially included Indonesians are active users of their accounts, the size of which increased significantly from 2014 to 2016.[①] However, the percentage of active users who had ever used an advanced service declined as the growth in active bank account users was not matched by the uptake of advanced services.

Bank account ownership drives Indonesian inclusive finance, and as one of the largest banks in Indonesia, Bank Rakyat Indonesia (BRI) has been playing an important role in promoting the financial inclusion in Indonesia with its specialization in small scale and microfinance. The example and model of BRI therefore will be analyzed in the following section.

6.1.2 Model of Bank Rakyat Indonesia (BRI)

Founded in 1896, BRI is currently the oldest and largest state-owned commercial bank in Indonesia (56.75% of state-owned shares and 43.25% of the public's shares). Looking at the total assets in 2016, it ranked as the first in Indonesia. Its main scope of business is financial services to agriculture and rural areas and foreign exchange business. In 1969, BRI set up credit departments at the village level to provide discount loans and to encourage the use of inputs such as fertilizers. From 1969 to 1983, the village credit departments did not have the independ-

① 2017 Annual Report: Financial Inclusion in Indonesia.

ent right to operate. They mainly acted as an agency to implement the business of a superior bank and did not have the qualifications to choose the prospective borrowers independently. The quality of credit services was poor, the rate of return was low, and the losses were serious.

In 1984, BRI lost a total of 23 million U.S. dollars and only 14% of village-level credit departments made profits. In order to overcome operational difficulties, improve economic efficiency and achieve self-financing, BRI carried out major structural reforms in more than 3,000 village-level credit departments. BRI changed the business agencies into independent business units, gained financial independence from government subsidies and set up good governance structure and information feedback mechanism, incentive mechanism and supervision mechanism, becoming a successful commercial bank.

In 1997, the Asian financial crisis swept through Southeast Asia, and many banks in Southeast Asia went bankrupt. However, the BRI's village-level credit departments remained profitable and saved BRI. In November 2003, BRI was listed on stock exchanges in Indonesia. Its business condition was far beyond the average level of commercial banks, with high return on assets and equity. Of the total loans of BRI, only 15% of them are lent by the village-level credit departments, which realized the majority of the total profits[1].

---

[1] Report on Indonesia's Financial Technology Development Report, CEResearch, 2017

Total Assets (Rp Billionl)   Loan-Gross (Rp Billionl)   Net Income for the Year (Rp Billionl)

Total Assets:
2012: 551,337
2013: 626,101
2014: 801,984
2015: 878,426
2016: 1,003,644

Loan-Gross:
2012: 362,007
2013: 448,345
2014: 510,697
2015: 581,095
2016: 663,420

Net Income for the Year:
2012: 18,687
2013: 21,354
2014: 24,227
2015: 25,411
2016: 26,228

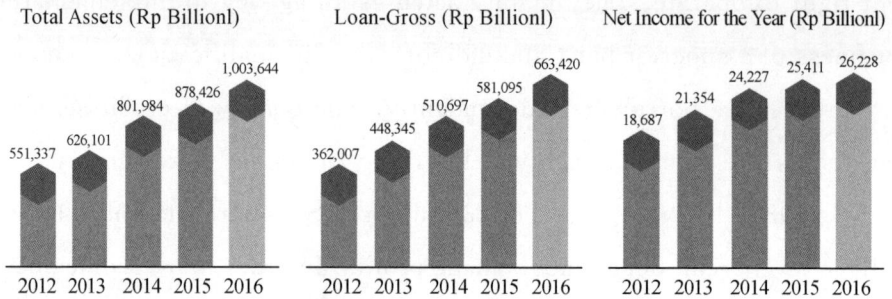

Source: Annual Report of BRI

Figure 6.2 Financial Index of BRI from 2012 to 2016

The target clients of BRI's microcredit business are individuals or small family workshops above the poverty line with good credit. The longest loan term is 2 years to 3 years. The use of the loans is limited to working capital or the purchase of fixed assets. The organizations of BRI can be divided into four levels. The first level is the bank headquarter in Jakarta. The second level is 15 regional branches. The third level is 320 sub-branches. The fourth level includes 3902 village credit departments located in rural areas. The village-level credit departments conduct business accounting independently, operate independently and assume full responsibility for their profits and losses. The village-level credit departments are usually located in the center of countryside villages and towns and serve as the most important part of BRI.

A typical credit department, usually covering 16 to 18 villages, has no more than 12 employees, 450 depositors and 70 loan clients. Employees have clear responsibilities and serve as managers, accountants, loan officers and salespersons. Four types of credit services are provided: corporate credit, medium-sized enterprise credit, small-sized enterprise credit and retail credit, as well as microcredit. The microcredit line is 5-5,000 U.S. dollars, and 87.9% of the microcredit loans are less than 30 U.S. dollars and do not require any collateral. Loan interest rates are generally 20% to 40%, and the repayment method is divided into two types: monthly repayment or installment repayment.

The main business model of the BRI's village credit departments is a four-level organizational structure, which includes a sound management system, a small credit department, moderate coverage, independent operation, independent accounting and clear division of labor, helping keep small but efficient operation. The BRI's village credit departments innovate financial products and ensure that the repayments are in full and on time through the deposit of the repayment system. Besides, they encourage early settlement by rebating the remaining interest.

The BRI's village credit departments have designed five kinds of savings products according to the needs of different depositors: institutions, urban residents, depositors who need medium liquidity pursue high yields, small depositors who need higher liquidity, and companies that pursue higher yields and farmers that are relatively rich. The BRI's village credit departments have designed demand-oriented financial products, offered credit products according to local conditions and implemented effective management and sound supervision, thus absorbing large amounts of savings and enriching BRI's sources of funds. The BRI's village-level credit departments have realized standardization and informatization of business: there are only five types of savings products and only one loan product.

Table 6.1 Financial Sustainability of BRI

		2011	2012	2013	2014	2015	2016
Indonesian People's Rural Bank Credit De-partment	Active loan	305.61	321.07	331.35	351.58	446.06	451.58
	Loan amount per capita/ GNIpc	—	57.37	56.09	62.30	59.36	42.13
	FSS	133.49	128.76	142.62	440.13	145.29	—
	ROE	108.11	95.98	117.52	108.47	127.39	—

* — no data yet

Source: www.mixmarket.org.

6.1.3 Policies and Regulations in Indonesia

Loose policies, prudential regulation, easy monetary policy and market-oriented interest rate reforms have rid BRI of government credit subsidies and improved the credit efficiency and liquidity of BRI, whose profits are able to cover the operating costs. Thus, BRI has achieved profitability as well as a sustainable development.

Through the course of the development of BRI, it is easy to see that Indonesia, a large developing country in Southeast Asia, has a-chieved great results through the model of state-owned banks. Indonesia has relaxed the control and regulation over interest rates, made flexible use of market mechanisms and served the poor. And Indonesia has standardized finance products and services and reduced the costs by uti-lizing the national network. This offers valuable experience to the inclu-sive finance in China's counties and rural areas. In China, there are also a number of large state-owned banks, which also have numerous bran-ches across the country. As long as the regulations on these state-owned banks are loosened and these state-owned banks are allowed to compete freely in the market, in the light of the experience of Indonesia, China will certainly make tremendous achievements in the county economy and rural economy in central regions and western regions of China.

At the same time, there are two major problems in the development of inclusive finance in Indonesia. First, the infrastructure and services of inclusive finance in Indonesia are insufficient, and the credit information system is incomplete. In Indonesia, only 6% of the total population are credit card holders. Second, new technology like mobile payment is not developed, resulting in the relatively high traditional costs, which will make the inclusive finance in Indonesia at a disadvantage in the future competition.

From the indicators of the sustainability of inclusive finance, the overall sustainability of inclusive financial institutions in Indonesia can not be quantified due to lack of data. Still, in terms of infrastructure, services and government regulation and policies, Indonesia's BRI is extremely successful, and its experience and lessons are worth for China to learn.

6.2 Development of Inclusive Finance in the Philippines

6.2.1 Economic Background of the Philippines

The Philippines was the first developing country in East Asia to embark on the road to industrialization. However, after the 1960s, the economic development of the Philippines showed the characteristics of "de-industrialization", the concrete manifestations of which were: low savings rate, low investment rate, low growth rate, weak export economy and stagnated rural development[①]. Since the 21st century, the Philippine government has taken a series of measures to achieve the economic transformation. However, various complicated economic factors and non-economic factors are intertwined, making the economic transformation of the Philippines difficult and uncertain.

From 2003 to 2007, the Philippine economy maintained a steady growth with a annual growth rate of 5%. In 2007, the Philippines enjoyed a rapid economic growth with a 7.1% increase in GDP (gross domestic product), the highest in 31 years. The total GDP of the Philippines was 144.6 billion U.S. dollars and the GDPPC (gross domestic product per capita) was 1,630 U.S. dollars. In 2008, under the influence of the U.S. recession, the Philippine economy was faced a huge challenge with a GDP of 168.6 billion U.S. dollars and an increase of 3. 8%.

After the financial crisis, the economy of the Philippines gradually recovered. In recent years, it has enjoyed a rapid growth with a growth rate of 6.1% in 2014, and 5.8% GDP growth rate in 2015, ranking the fourth in Asia, second only to China, India and Vietnam. In 2016, the growth rate of the Philippines was 6.92%, with a total GDP of 304.9 billion U.S. dollars, showing a good momentum of development.

One of the great advantages of the Philippines is the cheap and is the educated English-speaking workforce. The Philippines has a literacy rate of 94.6%, among the best in Asia. However, the Philippines is also troubled by problems such as political instability, corruption, outdated infrastructure and slow progress in legal reform. Various reforms ur-

---

① Shen Hongfang. Economic Transformation of the Philippines in the 21th Century: Difficulty and Challenges [J]. People's Tribune: Academic Frontier, 2017(1): 6—13.

gently needed by economic development are still under debate in parliament and the BOT program aimed at attracting private funds has only achieved limited success.

The 2016－2017 Global Competitiveness Report of the World Economic Forum shows that the Philippines ranked the 47th in the 134 most competitive countries around the world. Since 2012, the Philippine economy has shown steady growth with its GDP growth rate at around 5%. In 2016, the GDP of the Philippines was 14.48 trillion pesos (around US $ 340.9 billion at 51.29 pesos to 1 U.S. Dollar in 2016), an increase of 6.92% over the same period of the previous year. But the Philippines is still a relatively economically backward country in Southeast Asia. The Asian Development Bank predicts that the growth of the GDP of the Philippines will reach 7.3% in 2018.

In recent years, the Philippine government has tried hard to expand employment, and the unemployment rate of the Philippines is declining, which exceeded 8% in the Philippines between 2011 and 2014, and then reduced to 7% and 5.8% in 2015 and 2016 respectivel. The Philippines relies heavily on oil imports. In 2015, the international oil price met its downturn and the inflation rate in the Philippines was 1. 43%. In 2016, the inflation rate in the Philippines rebounded to 1.77%, but it was still higher than other countries and regions in ASEAN[①].

6.2.2 General Situation of Inclusive Finance in the Philippines

Accessing to inclusive financial services remains an important challenge especially in an archipelago comprising 7107 islands with a population of more than 92 million people. While there is a sustained increase

---

① Data from the Asian Development Bank

in the number of banks and ATMs, the distribution is highly skewed towards highly populous and urbanized areas. As of June 2017, there were 11343 banking offices and 19500 ATMs in the Philippines[①]. But banks and ATMs remained concentrated in NCR, CALARARZON and Central Luzon. As for other financial service access points, in 2016 there were over 61000 other financial service access points comprised credit cooperatives, microfinance NGOs, pawnshops, e-money agents, etc[②]. In the past 6 years, the average growth was highest among e-money agents and lowest among pawnshops.

Table 6.2 Geographic Distribution of Banks and ATMs in the Philippines

Region		Banks			ATMs		
		2015	2016	Growth (%)	2015	2016	Growth (%)
	NCR	3379	3504	3.7	7097	7669	8.1
	CAR	159	165	3.8	229	255	11.4
I	Ilocos Region	486	520	7.0	557	614	10.2
II	Cagayan Valley	347	358	3.2	296	354	19.6
III	Central Luzon	1088	1146	5.3	1569	1748	11.4
IV-A	CALABARZON	1621	1665	2.7	2566	2848	11.0
IV-B	MIMAROPA	246	267	8.5	221	250	13.1
V	Bicol Region	397	428	7.8	417	479	14.9
VI	Western Visayas	426	455	6.8	466	550	18.06
VII	Central Visayas	620	628	1.3	1197	1302	8.8

① Bangko Sentral ng Pilipinas, Report on the State of Financial Inclusion in the Philippines 2016.

② Http://www.bsp.gov.ph/ifas/listoffis dirsrch.asp

Continued

Region		Banks			ATMs		
		2015	2016	Growth (%)	2015	2016	Growth (%)
Ⅷ	Eastern Visayas	200	210	5.0	247	291	17.8
NIR	Negros Island Region	281	297	5.7	407	466	14.5
Ⅸ	Zamboanga Peninsula	215	220	2.3	254	291	14.6
Ⅹ	Northern Mindanao	376	383	1.9	454	497	9.5
ⅩⅠ	Davao Region	408	424	3.9	708	776	9.6
ⅩⅡ	SOCCSKSARGEN	222	232	4.5	363	396	9.1
ⅩⅢ	Caraga	218	208	−4.6	233	260	11.6
	ARMM	21	19	−9.5	33	35	6.1
	Philippines	10710	11129	3.9	17314	19081	10.2
	Top 3 Bottom3						

Source: Report on the State of Financial Inclusion in the Philippines 2016.

As for the usage of inclusive finance, the 2009 Consumer Financial Survey suggested that only 2 out of 10 Filipino households have a deposit account in a formal financial situation. Data from the World Bank 2011 Findex indicate that only 20.5% of Filipino adults had a loan from a formal financial institution in the past year[①]. These gaps present both a challenge and opportunity to ensure that access translates into effective usage of available products and services. From 2011 to 2016, the number of deposit accounts and depositors in banks increased at an average annual rate of 4% and 6% respectively. Geographically speaking, NCR held more that 40% of the total number of deposit accounts, fol-

---

① Financial Inclusion in the Philippines, Issued No. 1, First Quarter 2013.

lowed by CALABARZON and Central Luzon. In terms of amount, deposits were heavily concentrated in NCR which accounted for more than two-thirds of the total.

6.2.3 Model of Inclusive Financial in the Philippines

The inclusive financial institutions in the Philippines are mainly divided into three types: NGOs, banks and cooperatives.

Table 6.3 Inclusive Financial Institutions in the Philippines in 2015

Type	NGO	Bank	Cooperative
Number	18	176	14739
Loan balance (10,000 peso)	42300	1140000	—
Number of borrowers	13268	1230000	6800000

* — no data yet

Source: www.adb.org

Center for Agriculture and Rural Development (CARD) is the earliest and largest NGO conducting microfinance business in the Philippines, the business of which has reached 40 provinces. In 1997, CARD set up savings-based rural banks to enable impoverished rural women to put some of their microfinance profits in the banks and to stabilize the family economy. At the same time, Filipino women operate a type of community store called Sari-sari store through CARD's microfinance. Sari-sari means "diversified" in the Filipino language. This store is mainly distributed in urban and rural residential areas and has become an important cultural symbol in the Philippines. CARD supports the entrepreneurial work of poor women in the Philippines through Sari-sari stores and also utilizes the Sari-sari store network to establish the company Hapinoy. Hapinoy is a compound word of Happy and Pinoy, referring to a happy Filipino. Hapinoy is a small and micro enterprise development project conducted by CARD as well as an enterprise established to solve social problems such as poverty. To help married Filipino women become small and micro entrepreneurs running Sari-sari stores, Hapinoy provides them with related courses, necessary capital and opportunities. When promoting the development of inclusive finance, China should also pay attention to the cooperation with local non-government organizations to carry out poverty alleviation work and to create economic and social values.

Considering the supply and coverage of inclusive finance, banks and cooperatives are the main providers of inclusive financial services in the Philippines, and because there are no datum providing for Philippine cooperatives, the supply and coverage of inclusive finance is incomplete. According to the introduction in the World Association of Microfinance Alliance Meeting on November 29 by Robert Alan from Philippine microfinance coalition[1], cooperatives in the Philippines have already covered 30% of the Philippines population.

From the perspective of inclusive financial demand in the Philippines, the major demand for inclusive financial services in the Philippines is also to provide basic agricultural means of production, to conduct post-disaster funding plans after natural disasters such as typhoons[2], as well as to improve the basic living conditions of the people.

The Philippines has already abolished the government's direct in-

---

[1] http://bank.hexun.com/2016-12-04/187188895.html.

[2] The Philippines is a typhoon center, and the country is usually attacked by typhoons twenty-five to thirty times a year.

volvement in credit projects. It is the microcredit institutions rather than the government that take a leading role in microcredit business. In the Philippines, microfinance is at the core of poverty alleviation and the Philippines recognizes microfinance as a legitimate banking business. In 2011, the Philippines proposed microfinance as a national strategy and stated that microfinance was one of the pillars of inclusive finance. The Philippines has set up special supervisory organizations and cooperative development agencies for cooperatives.

The Philippines has proposed a micro-regulatory commission to certify the standardization of cooperatives so as to ensure that the cooperatives meet certain standards in terms of cooperative governance, financial performance and social performance. Besides, the Philippines has also stipulated that transparency and information disclosure of cooperatives should satisfy certain criteria.

At the same time, in order to encourage inclusive finance, the Philippines has granted a 2% tax credit on the total tax for microfinance and required protection for providers and demanders of inclusive finance. In terms of government administration and legislation, Philippine government administration is at the forefront of the world and is relatively complete.

The financial infrastructure in the Philippines was relatively backward until the Philippines began to consciously conduct the construction of a comprehensive credit information system in 2016, in which banks and cooperatives were required to submit relevant data to the credit bureaus for the evaluation and analyses of the credit of the citizens.

6.3 Path Selection: Drawing Lesson from Indonesia and the Philippines

Inclusive financial from Indonesia and Philippines is improving significantly, but there are still many difference between the Philippines and Indonesia. The following table shows the detail in term of using inclusive finance CGAP frame work.

Table 6.4 Comparison between Indonesia and the Philippines

	Indonesia	The Philippines
Provider	Independent branches of state-owned banks	Major community banks; cooperatives
Demander	Poor people in urban and rural areas	Poor people in urban and rural areas
Financial Infrastructure	Backward payment system; incomplete credit system	Backward payment system
Government Regulation	Lenient	Normative; incentive; comprehensive
2016—2017 Global Competitiveness	#37	#47
2016 GDPPC (U.S. Dollar)	3570	2951
Proportion of Poverty	10.9%	21.6%

Source: www.adb.org

Prudently learning from the experience and lessons of Indonesia and the Philippines will have a positive effect on the sustainable development of inclusive finance in China. However, the implementation of systems, policies and the selection of an inclusive financial model can not be done by simply analogizing and copying other countries' models. China should take full consideration of its actual situation and find the most suitable way for the development of inclusive finance in China.

After basic analysis and comparison among the development of inclusive finance in China and Indonesia and the Philippines, the path selection for China's sustainable inclusive finance has been quite obvious based on the development practice and common issues of global inclusive finance.

(1)China's inclusive finance should be systematically sustainable. It should take into account not only the financial sustainability to be achieved by financial institutions as providers, but also the sustainability on the demand side so as to achieve the systematical balance between supply and demand and sustainable development.

(2)Compared with two Southeast Asian countries, China's inclusive finance started relatively late but is developing rapidly and possesses the late-mover advantages, which means that it can borrow the experience from other countries and avoid the same governance, legal or risk issues.

(3)China's inclusive finance is developed under strong national influence and is part of the overall national strategy. This is an external condition which other countries do not have. Therefore, the state is supposed to play a bigger role in the the promotion and deepening of inclusive finance through popularizing new inclusive financial instruments, especially insurance and new electronic payment instruments, and try to maximize the late-mover advantages.

(4)The sustainability of inclusive finance in China is realized in the rapid development of China's macro economy and in the process of achieving urbanization. Therefore, China's inclusive finance shonld meet the needs of urbanization and must take the reality and dynamic changes of urban-rural dual structure into consideration. For example, a demander of inclusive finance may change from a farmer to an urban resident overnight. Thus, in achieving the sustainability of inclusive finance in China, changes in this dynamic environment needs to be paid more attention to.

Chapter 7　Conclusion and Suggestions

7.1 Sustainability of Inclusive Finance under China's Specific National Conditions

China's inclusive finance plays an extremely important role in promoting China's urbanization, since it has accelerated the process of urbanization in China and will accompany the whole process of urbanization. Therefore, an important factor in the sustainability of China's inclusive finance is the inclusive financial support needed by China's urbanization.

In China, the local banks, of which the majority are in the eastern coastal cities, find it difficult to meet the funding requirements of different forms of ownership, reflecting the issue of regional imbalance. At the same time, a socialist market economy is still under construction, the urbanization is still under way, and the problems of the urban-rural dual structure still exist. In this context, inclusive financial services inevitably show features of different nationalities, stages and structures.

Therefore, the main problem of China's inclusive finance is how to achieve sustainable development, avoid risk and provide high-quality services in the context of the existing urban-rural dual structure, the process of urbanization and the unique socialist market economy.

The urban-rural dual structure is formed in history. Inclusive finance acknowledges this context and attempts to improve the unbalanced distribution of financial resources caused by the urban-rural dual structure and solve the issue of financial repression through its efforts and development. It should be noticed that inclusive finance provides financial services based on the individual subject in the urban-rural dual structure, that is, the actual gap between urban and rural areas and between the East and the West of China. The purpose of inclusive financial services is still to promote the gradual elimination of the urban-rural dual structure through urbanization while satisfying the financial needs.

In the process of urbanization, the development of the secondary, tertiary industries and the urban agglomeration are promoted, rural labor force is transferred, an urbanization system centering on industrialization is formed, and the overall labor productivity is improved[1], which will raise the overall income level, lower the proportion of primary industry, achieve a relatively modest rate of employment in primary industry and increase the income of the remaining primary industry employees so as to narrow the income gap caused by the urban-rural dual structure and get rid of the restrictions of financial repression and financial exclusion.

Therefore, inclusive finance, while respecting reality and providing inclusive financial services, should always remember the goal of promoting urbanization throughout its whole process. Specifically, with the development in counties and farms, inclusive finance should pay attention to the goal of dynamic urbanization and continue to serve the needs of rural inclusive finance when entering the urbanized market structure.

---

① Xia Geng, Study on the Transformation of Urban-rural Dual Economic Structure in China[M]. Peking University Press, 48.

7.2 Suggestions

7.2.1 Establishing Multi-agent Provider Competition Mechanism

Multi-agent provider competition means that a variety of inclusive financial models develop while complementing each other in the multi-level inclusive financial system. Inclusive financial services mainly focus on low-income groups, and promoting inclusive financial services, all regions and social groups with financial needs including the poor, low-income earners and SMEs. At present, China's financial system is aimed at middle and high-end markets and is relatively complete. However, the financial supply for low-income groups in rural and urban areas is still insufficient, and solving this issue is the key to the success of inclusive financial system. The diversity of demander groups has determined the importance of developing different models of inclusive finance based on local conditions.

Commercial microcredit, with gaining profits as its main principle, focuses on profits and risk aversion. It can achieve sustainable development only with clients possessing a large sum of funds. Policy-based microcredit has nonprofit characteristics and can provide subsidies and loans with low interest rates to the poor through poverty alleviation funds. However, this type of credit relies too much on external funds and policy support, which is difficult to achieve sustainability. Therefore, only by developing a multi-model financial system can the needs of different classes and different demander groups be satisfied as well as the basic requirements of building an inclusive financial system be met. To this end, regular financial institutions should be encouraged to further participate in the development of inclusive finance. The experience of the BPI model shows that, formal financial institutions' profits through inclusive financial services can be equal to those through formal financial services.

From the above analysis of the potential demanders of inclusive finance in China, it can be seen that China's urban and rural economy is developing rapidly, individual enterprises and small-scale township enterprises who have great development potential as well as a strong demand for funds, are emerging in the society. Therefore, providing financial services to these vulnerable groups actively can be a growth pole for formal financial institutions in achieving sustainable development.

7.2.2 Strengthening the Construction of Financial Infrastructure and Optimizing Social Assistance 2System

The government should strengthen the construction of financial infrastructure, especially in rural areas and poor urban areas, and should improve the overall level of financial services in these regions through measures such as increasing the coverage of ATMs and improving payment and settlement services. At the same time, it is necessary to create a sound financial environment in the society that includes the credit environment, a guarantee system and an insurance system.

At present, the construction of credit investigation system in urban areas is carried out well. In the vast rural areas, China should fully utilize the advantages of rural credit cooperative branches and the late-mover advantages of the Internet and big data to comprehensively promote the construction of credit investigation of individuals and township enterprises. Institutions should collect credit information of all kinds of SMEs and villagers, set up credit information database in the credit investigation system of the People's Bank of China and the credit sharing mechanism, and improve the capital operation efficiency in the inclusive financial system.

For the credit loans provided to microcredit clients and township enterprises in rural areas, China should establish a variety of insurance mechanisms to divert the natural and market risks as well as a diversified and multi-level credit guarantee system, which China should further support by introducing certain agriculture-related financial funds so as to solve the problem of farmers' and township enterprises' poor access to loans as soon as possible.

At the same time, it is necessary to establish and improve the social assistance system of inclusive finance such as rating agencies, trade associations, credit bureaus, settlement and payment systems and professional financial service networks. It is essential to establish China's network system of inclusive financial projects and to provide timely information, monitoring and tracking of financial products.

7.2.3 Promoting Diversity and Full Coverage of Financial Services

Seen from the operational mechanism, financial institutions should innovate and design diversified financial products and provide not only microcredit services but also other financial services to meet the clients' increasing needs for inclusive finance. For example, branches of institutions can provide services such as payment and settlement services, fund management services and pension savings in rural areas and expand the variety and scope of financial services by constantly improving the service level of intermediaries.

As early as 2008, the People's Bank of China announced that the existing banks, loan companies, rural mutual financial cooperative and other microfinance institutions were allowed to perform payment and settlement services[①]. However, until now, the majority of inclusive financial services in China are still mainly microcredit services, and the types of financial services are limited, which can no longer meet the diversified needs of residents in urban and rural areas. Therefore, in the development process of financial institutions, efforts should be intensified at promoting intermediary businesses and clients should be provided with various financial products such as funds and insurance. At the same time, China must continue to explore suitable inclusive financial services for low-income groups.

7.2.4 Promoting Urbanization and Transforming the Urban-rural Dual Structure

China should achieve the sustainable development of inclusive finance by establishing a modern inclusive financial system and achieving integrative development of financial service. Many overseas scholars have carried out empirical research to prove the close relationship between economic development and financial support, and it is clear that establishing a sustainable integrative financial development service system can not only enabled people of all classes to enjoy convenient financial services but also serve as an important part in realizing the "13th Five-Year Plan". To establish a sustainable inclusive financial system, the government's support and supervision is needed. Besides that, the institutions themselves should pay more attention to the prevention of

---

① People's Bank of China No. 11, 2008.

risks and actively expand the channels for operating funds so as to reduce their dependence on government support and poverty alleviation funds.

In rural areas, China should establish a rural capital inflow mechanism through motivation and compensation and minimize the outflow of rural capital. At the same time, in order to realize the sustainable development of modern inclusive finance, full attention should be paid to controlling the credit risk on the demand side, improving the ability of early risk warning and reducing the rate of bad loans. Main demanders of inclusive financial services are low-income groups with low education level and poor credit concept. Therefore, financial institutions that provide financial services to such groups should fully understand their actual production, living conditions and credit conditions, and the government should, together with the financial institutions, provide a resource-sharing credit rating system for farmers, establish a credit investigation system, strengthen the risk control and identification capabilities of business personnel and enhance the cooperation with insurance agencies and other agencies to transfer risks and enhance risk tolerance. Only through strengthening risk prevention and improving operating efficiency can China achieve the sustainable development of inclusive finance and establish an inclusive financial development system that meets the requirements of modern finance.

In the meantime, in the process of building China's inclusive financial system, China must provide the financial services needed by financial demanders according to China's national conditions and geographical features, and established a inclusive financial system with China's characteristics based on successful experience of foreign models. China should focus on the sustainable development of inclusive finance and attach great importance to the control over profits and risks of financial institutions that provide inclusive financial services and correspondingly establish a risk control system so that the entire financial services can be shared at an early date and comprehensive financial support can be provided to economic construction and social development.

7.3 Outlook

The sustainability of China's inclusive finance has developed rapidly in recent years, the reason of which is that the inherent laws of inclusive finance are in line with China's reality and the two have worked together. In the vigorous urbanization process, the reform from financial repression to financial deepening and the gradual transformation of urban-rural dual structure in China will undoubtedly play an extremely important role, showing historical significance in the construction and development of China's inclusive financial system. It is the very purpose of this paper to study the issue of the sustainable development of inclusive finance in China by drawing lessons and experience from other countries.

From the development of capital, it can be seen that the role of finance in human society is becoming more and more important. The essence of inclusive finance is to ensure that every individual obtains the financial services he/she needs and deserves. In the past, inclusive finance mainly focused on providing services to the poor excluded from adequate financial services. In the future, even if poverty is eliminated, the relatively poor and vulnerable groups will still exist and inclusive finance will still be meaningful and indispensable with its essence unchanged.

China is a socialist country, and the ideals of inclusive finance and socialism are identical. Thus inclusive finance will surely enjoy sustainable development in China, which is in line with the general requirements on improving the socialist market economy, as in the 19th CPC National Congress, General Secretary Xi Jinping stated in the reports that, "We will deepen institutional reform in the financial sector, make it better to serve the real economy, to increase the proportion of direct financing, and to promote the healthy development of a multilevel capital market. China will improve the framework of regulation underpinned by monetary policy and macro-prudential policy, and see that interest rates and exchange rates become more market-based. China will improve the financial regulatory system to forestall systemic financial risks.[①]"

The sustainable development of inclusive finance is based on the operation system composed of people with diversified interests and on the stakeholders with cooperation and mutual trust, which is realized in the Pareto improvement under the benefit-compatible value system through win-win cooperation. The ideal inclusive financial system is essentially coordinated with the socialist system in China. Therefore, the inclusive financial system in China should be sustainable although various problems will arise in the development process, (because it will gradually develop through improvement and enjoy joint development with the inclusive nature of socialism.)

The sustainability of inclusiveness is the result of the coordination between financial theories and social development. China has provided a

---

[①] http://finance.sina.com.cn/roll/2017-10-19/doc—ifymvuyt4552326.shtml.

practical platform for the development of inclusive finance. At the same time, China carried out inclusive financial practice to promote its urbanization and modernization so as to change the urban-rural dual structure and realize the inclusiveness of inclusive finance. This is the realistic value of this paper's study on the sustainability of inclusive finance.

Bibliography

Ai, Luming. 2000. *Microcredit and poverty alleviation* [M]. Beijing: Economic Science Press.

Abdel, R. 2008. Arab microfinance analysis and benchmarking report [R].

Bai, Qinxian. 2001. *Introduction to research on sustainable financial development* [M]. China Finance Publishing House.

Bei, Duoguang., & Li, Yan. 2016. *New area of digital inclusive finance* [M]. Beijing: People's Publishing House.

Bei, Duoguang. 2017. *National development strategy for inclusive finance: 2016 report on the development of inclusive finance* [M]. Beijing: Economic Management Press.

Cao, Shu. 2004. *Research on poverty relief and development in Dingxi* [M]. China Social Sciences Publishing House.

Chang, Ge. 2015. *Research on the sustainable development of village banks in China* [M]. Beijing: Economic Management Press.

Chen, Yulu., & Ma, Yong. 2015. *Outline of China's rural economy* [M]. Beijing: China Finance Publishing House.

Cheng, Enjiang., & Liu, Xichuan. 2007. *Non—governmental microcredit and rural finance in China* [M]. Zhejiang University Press.

Cheng, Siwei. 2005. *Reform and development: Promoting China's inclusive finance* [M]. Beijing: Economic Science Press.

Cheng, Huixia. 2009. *Sustainable development and financial ecol-*

ogy of small and medium institutions [M]. Beijing Normal University Press.

Robert, C., & Thomas, U. 1991. *Law and economics* [M]. Shanghai: Shanghai Branch of Sanlian Bookstore.

Dai, Hongwei., & Sui, Zhikuan. 2014. Construction and latest development of China's inclusive financial system [J]. *Theory Journal*, 2014(5).

Deng, Li., & Ran, Guanghe. 2006. Research on coordinated development mechanism of rural finance and rural economy [J], *Productivity Research*, 2006 (3), 32−34.

Dong, Xiaolin., & Zhu, Minjie. 2016. Supply−side reform of rural finance and construction of inclusive financial system [J], *Journal of Nanjing Agricultural University (Social Science Edition)*, 2016 (6), 14−18

Dong, Yanling. 2005. *Research on bank credit and financing of SMEs* [M]. Beijing: Economic Science Press.

Du, Xiaoshan. 2006. Development of microcredit and framework of inclusive financial system [J]. *Chinese Rural Economy*.

Du, Xiaoshan. 2007. Building a sustainable rural inclusive financial system [J]. *Finance and Economy*.

Du, Xingjun. 2013. System construction of rural inclusive finance in Taiwan [J]. *Journal of Hunan University (Social Science Edition)*.

Du, Xiaoshan., & You, Qiang. 2015. Cooperation of financial institutions in the field of microcredit [J]. *Rural Finance Research*.PH

Du, Zhaoyun. 2016. *Theory and practice of inclusive finance* [M]. Xiamen: Xiamen University Press.

Engels Compilation and Translation Bureau of the CPC Central Committee, 2012. *Selected works of Marx and Engels (Vol. 4)* [M].

Beijing: People's Publishing House.

Fuller, D. 1998. Credit union development: financial inclusion and exclusion [J]. *Geoforum*, 29(2), 145—157.

George, C., Xu, Lixin., Colin., & Zou Hengfu. 2003. Finance income inequality: test of alternative theories [R]. World Bank Policy Research Working Paper, 29—84.

Guo, Xingping. 2010. Research on rural inclusive financial system based on E—financial service innovation [J]. *Finance and Trade Economics*.

He, Sijiang., Yan, Gujun,. & Chen, Kuihua. 2013. *Microfinance: theory and practice* [M]. Hangzhou: Zhejiang University Press.

He, Weida., & Yang SHihui. 1998. *Modern western theories of property rights* [M]. Beijing: Chinese Financial and Economic Publishing House.

Helms, B. 2006. *Access for all* [M], World Bank Publications.

Holmes F. 2002. The role of central banks in microfinance in Asia and the Pacific [J]. *Asian—pacific Economic Literature*, 16(1), 54 - 55.

Hong, S. N. 2004. Efficiency and effectiveness of microfinance in Vietnam: Evidence from NGO schemes in north and central regions [J]. *CEPA, School of Economics*.

Hong, Xuefeng., & Wang, Zhijiang. 2009. Empirical analysis of the relation between China's income gap and financial development [J]. *Statistics and Decision*, 2009(9), 135—136.

Hu, Guohui., & Wang, Jing. 2015. *Financial exclusion and construction of inclusive financial system: Theory and China's practice* [M]. Beijing: China Finance Publishing House.

Jiang, Zhaogang. 2005. *Comprehensive competitiveness of county economy* [M]. Beijing: Economic Science Press.

Jiao, Jinpu,. & Wang, Aijian. 2015. *Inclusive finance: Basic principles and China's practice* [M]. Beijing: China Finance Publishing House.

Jiao, Jinpu., & Chen, Jin. 2009. *Building China's inclusive financial system : Providing opportunities and approaches for all people to enjoy modern financial services* [M]. Beijing: China Finance Publishing House.

Lapenu, Z. 2003. Measuring social performance of microfinance institutions: A proposal [J]. *Argidius Foundation and Consultative Group to Assist the Poorest.*

Li, Jianjun 2005. *Scale of underground finance in China and its impact on macro economy* [M]. Beijing: China Finance Publishing House.

Li, Yaxin. 2002. Sticking to the direction of serving agriculture, farmers and rural areas: research on rural cooperatives in Yinping county [J], *Chinese Rural Economy*, 2002 (12) , 73—75

Liang, Shen., & Zhu Bowen. 2014. Current situation and implication of research on inclusive finance: From the perspective of microcredit [J]. *Journal of Central University of Finance and Economics.*

Lietaer, B. 2003. *The future of currency* [M]. Beijing: Xinhua Publishing House.

Luo, Enping. 2005. Research on general characteristics and development tendency of rural financial demand [J]. *Fujian Forum (Humanity and Social Science Edition)*, 2005(9), 20—23.

Luo, Jun. 2010. *Development on cooperative finance* [M]. Sichuan University Press.

Mix. 2008. Asia Microfinance analysis and bench marking report

[R].

Mustafa, S. 1996. *Beacon of hope: An impact assessment of BRAC's rural development programme* [M]. Dhaka: University Press.

Ndii, D. 2004. Role and development of microfinance and savings and credit cooperatives in Africa [R].

Nieto. 2007. Microfinance institutions and efficiency [J]. *The International Journal of Management Science.*

Pang, Jiying., & Zhang, Jianhua. 2008. *Market—exit issue of financial institutions* [M]. Beijing: China Finance Publishing House.

Questionnaire Survey Analysis Group on Farmer Lending of People's Bank of China. 2009. *Questionnaire survey report on farmer lending* [M]. Beijing: Economic Science Press.

Robert, M, T., & Ueda, K. 2003. Financial deepening, inequality, and growth: A model — based quantitative evaluation [R]. IMF Working Paper.

Robinson. 2004. Why the Bank Rakyat Indonesia has the world's largest sustainable microbanking System [R], Paper presented at BRI International Seminar.

Shen, Hongfang. 2002. *Comparative study on development model of East Asian economy* [M]. Xiamen: Xiamen University Press.

Shen, Hongfang. 2008. *Economic globalization and economic security: Experience and lessons of East Asia* [M]. Beijing: China Economic Publishing House.

Shen Hongfang, Economic Transformation of the Philippines in the 21th Century: Difficulty and Challenges [J]. *People's Tribune: Academic Frontier*, 2017(1): 6—13.

Shen, Jie., & Ma Jiujie. 2010. Research on the development of

China's new rural financial institutions [J]. *Economic Review*.

Shen, Kai. 2008. *Study on SME credit guarantee system* [M]. Intellectual Property Publishing House.

Shi, Ce. 2015. *Graphical internet finance* [M]. Beijing: Chemical Industry Press.

Song, Yu. 2016. *Development path of inclusive finance: From the perspective of SMEs* [M]. Beijing: Economic Science Press.

Tan, Wenpei. 2013. Construction of rural inclusive financial system: From the perspective of "trinity" [J]. *Journal of Hunan University (Social Science Edition)*.

Tapscott, D. 2016. *Economics in the age of data: Rethinking opportunities and risks in the network intelligence era* [M]. Beijing: Mechanical Industry Press.

Tian, Bao. 2011. *Study on the issues of financial support for county economic development* [M]. Lanzhou University Press.

UNDP. 2006. Building inclusive financial sectors for development [R].

Wang, Xiaoya. 2014. *Rural financial reform: Key field and basic approaches* [M]. Beijing: China Finance Publishing House.PH

Wang, Qin. 1995. *Research on the development of Singapore's economy* [M]. Xiamen: Xiamen University Press.

Wang, Huaiyong. 2014. Innovation of rural financial regulatory concept and its exploration and practice: From the rise of rural microfinance [J]. *Social Science Research*.

Wei, Shengwen. 2009. Anti−poverty [M]. Social Sciences Academic Press.

Wen, Tao. 2010. *Study on service innovation and dynamic competition strategy of rural financial sustainable development* [M]. Beijing: Beijing Normal University University Press.

Wu, Chongbo. 2011. *Contemporary research on Indonesia's economy* [M]. Xiamen: Xiamen University Press.

Wu, Guohua. 2013. Further improvement of rural inclusive financial system in China [J]. *Comparative Economic and Social Systems*.

Wu, Xiaoling., & Jiao, jinpu. 2011. *China microcredit blue book* [M]. Beijing: Economic Science Press..

Wu, Zhongchao. 2013. *Sustainable growth of China's rural commercial banks: Measurement and evaluation* [M]. Beijing: China Social Sciences Publishing House.

Xie, Chi., Sun, Bai., & Wang, Shouyang. 2009. *Study on financial support for new rural construction* [M]. Changsha: Hunan University Press.

Xie, Ping., & Chen, Chao., & Chen, Xiaowen. 2015. *China P2P internet loans: Market, Institutions and business models* [M]. Beijing: China Finance Publishing House.

Xin, Yao. 2010. *Research on rural lending in less developed areas* [M]. Shanghai: Shanghai Branch of Sanlian Bookstore.

Xu, Xiaobo. 1994. *Reform and development of rural finance in China* [M]. Beijing: Contemporary China Publishing House.

Xu, Xiaobo., & Deng, Yingtao. 1994. *Reform and development of rural finance in China* 1979—1990 [M]. Beijing: Contemporary China Publishing House.

Yang, Jun., Li, Xiaoyu., & Zhang, Zongye. 2006. Empirical analysis on the level of financial development and residents' income in China [J]. *Economic Science*, 2006(2), 23—33.

Yang, Zhaoting., & Ma, Yanli. 2013. *Research on the coordination of rural financial supply and demand* [M]. Beijing: China Finance Publishing House.

Yao, Yaojun. 2006. Empirical analysis of the relationship between financial development and urban and rural income gap [J]. *Journal of Finance and Economics*, 2005(2), 49—59.

Yaron J. 1997. Rural finance: Issues, design, and best practices [J]. *Work in Progress for Public Discussion*.

Yin, Chen., & Ling, Feng. 2013. *Research on the sustainable development of China's rural banks* [M]. Shanghai: Fudan University Press.

Yin, Wanghui., Ming, Yue., & Pu, Yongjian. 2008. Research and analysis of China's rural microcredit institutions under inclusive financial system [J]. *Journal of Chongqing University (Social Science Edition)*.

Zhang, Lijun., & Zhan, Yong. 2006. The impact of rural financial development on income differences between urban and rural areas in China: Test based on the 1978—2001 data [J]. *Journal of Central University of Finance and Economics*.

Zhang, Zhengping. 2013. *Research on the sustainable development of China's microfinance institutions* [M]. Beijing: Economic Science Press.

Zhang, Zhengping. 2016. *Commercialization of microfinance institutions, risk and target deviation: Theory and evidence* [M]. Beijing: China Finance Publishing House.

Zhang, Zhiyuan. 2009. *Theory of regional financial sustainable development: From the perspective of institutions* [M]. Science Press.

Zheng, Zhonghua., & Te, Riwen. 2014. China's dual financial structure and construction of inclusive financial system [J]. *Macroeconomic Study*.

Zhong, Wei. 2007. *Evaluation and analysis of China's sustainable financial development* [M]. Beijing: Economic Science Press.

Zhou, Guoliang. 2007. Analysis of causes and harm of shortage in rural finance supply [J], *Development and Research*, 2007 (2), 61—64.

Zhou, Mengliang., & Zhang, Guozheng. 2009. A new reform method of rural financial reform in China from the perspective of inclusive finance [J]. *Journal of Central University of Finance and Economics*.

Zhu, Jialin. 2016. *New economy, new finance* [M]. Beijing: China Citic Press.

Zou, Lixing. 2013. *Open economy and sustainable development* [M]. Changsha: Hunan University Press.